Library of
Davidson College

My Conversations
with
Teilhard de Chardin
on the
Primacy of Christ

MY CONVERSATIONS WITH TEILHARD DE CHARDIN ON THE PRIMACY OF CHRIST

Peking, 1942-1945

GABRIEL M. ALLEGRA, O. F. M.
President of the Franciscan Biblical Institute

Translated with an Introduction and Notes
by
BERNARDINO M. BONANSEA, O. F. M.
*Professor of Philosophy
Catholic University of America*

FRANCISCAN HERALD PRESS
CHICAGO, ILLINOIS

COPYRIGHT © 1971 BY FRANCISCAN HERALD PRESS
1434 W. 51st STREET, CHICAGO, ILLINOIS 60609
LIBRARY OF CONGRESS CATALOG CARD NUMBER: 72-129246
ISBN: 8199-0429-5

Imprimi potest:
    BARTHOLOMEW BENGISSER, O. F. M.
        Commissary of the Holy Land

Nihil obstat:
    JOHN JOSEPH MANNING, O. F. M.
        Censor deputatus

Imprimatur:
    ✝ LAWRENCE B. CASEY
        Bishop of Paterson

July 17, 1970

PRINTED IN THE UNITED STATES OF AMERICA

ACKNOWLEDGMENTS

The translator wishes to express his sincere gratitude to the Right Reverend John K. Ryan, Ph.D., LL. D., former dean of the School of Philosophy of the Catholic University of America, for his reading the manuscript and his many helpful suggestions; to the Reverend Romano S. Almagno, O. F. M., for writing the Preface to this work; and to the staff of St. Anthony Guild Press for their professional assistance in the final preparation of this volume.

He also wishes to thank the publishers listed below for permitting him to quote from the works indicated. The folios in parentheses indicate the pages in this book on which the quotations are to be found.

Holt, Rinehart, and Winston, Inc., New York, N. Y., Dante Alighieri, *The Divine Comedy*, translated by H. R. Huse, copyright © 1954, by H. R. Huse. (pp. 52-53, 58, 85-86, 98); Darton, Longman, and Todd, Ltd., and Doubleday and Co., Inc., *The Jerusalem Bible*, copyright © 1966 (pp. 57, 67-68, 84, 106); the Confraternity of Christian Doctrine *New Testament*, copyright 1941 (pp. 61, 69, 79).

PREFACE

Each year in the July-December issue of the Historical Archives of the Society of Jesus, there is a section devoted to a bibliography of the Society's history, wherein are listed any and all publications in any way pertinent to the subject. Since 1955, the year of Teilhard's death, the section of the "Bibliographia" under his name has continually grown; so much so that in the latest issue numbers 536-685 (i. e., pp. 591-601) are entirely devoted to Teilhardian literature.

Literature by and about Teilhard de Chardin continues to flood the literary markets of Europe, America, and the Third World. Most recently, for example, *The Future of Man* was translated into Japanese by Itō Akira and Watanabe Yoshinaru and published by Misuzu-Shobō in Japan.

Despite severe criticism in certain areas of the Roman Catholic Church, Teilhard is still, as John Kobler wrote, "The Priest Who Haunts the Catholic World." And some of the very best Roman Catholic scholars have not only commented on Teilhard's life and work, but have used his writings as the very springboard for their speculation.

Of course, not everything published on Teilhard is of the scholarly caliber that serious Teilhardian study deserves and demands. As Henri de Lubac has stated, Teilhard has often been hurt by friends and admirers because of superficial scholarship. It becomes, therefore, the task of those involved in Teilhardiana to sift the wheat from the chaff, the scholar from the fan, and the good work from the poor study.

Happily, the present volume which records and recalls the association and conversation of Pierre Teilhard de Chardin, S. J., and Gabriel M. Allegra, O. F. M., falls heavily on the positive side of excellent and exceptional Teilhardiana. This volume is not only important because it affords a valuable insight into a period in Teilhard's life which up to now (despite the marvelous work of Cuénot and Speaight) has been somewhat hidden and veiled, but also because it *answers some very important questions* and gives us a privileged insight into the very core of Teilhard's soul.

For a long while now, scholars have sensed a certain similarity, connection, or even dependence between the Christological thought of the Franciscan Doctor John Duns Scotus and of Pierre Teilhard de Chardin. The Belgian Capuchin N. Max Wildiers, general editor of the official French edition of Teilhard's complete works, has noted — in his book *An Introduction to Teilhard de Chardin* — the unity between the Scotistic and Teilhardian interpretation of Christ. Christopher Mooney, S. J., in his masterful work *Teilhard de Chardin and the*

Mystery of Christ, has also seen this unity, but stresses the importance of underlining both the contrasts and the similarity.

Yet, despite the insights of Wildiers, Mooney, de Lubac, and others, the question as to any connection between Scotus and Teilhard still remained unanswered. Did Teilhard ever study the thought of John Duns Scotus? If so, was he influenced by Scotus as was, for example, Gerard Manley Hopkins? Father Allegra's book gives an answer to these important questions — and in the affirmative! Teilhard, under the aegis of Allegra, not only studied and admired John Duns Scotus, but came to see similarities between his ideas and those of the medieval Franciscan. Furthermore, Teilhard was so impressed with Scotistic thought that he called it: "... *la théologie cosmique, la théologie de l'avenir.*"

With all of this stated and proved — an important question is answered by this volume. Likewise, an accusation leveled against Teilhard is defeated. Teilhard is often accused of being a poor theologian, and this because he lacked professional training (as a student) and professional guidance (as a writer). In *My Conversations with Teilhard de Chardin on the Primacy of Christ* we see Teilhard investigating Scripture, patristic sources, and Franciscan documents under the direction of Allegra, who (as Father Bonansea points out in his *Introduction*) is known for his vast learning and fault-

PREFACE

less scholarship. Teilhard may not have been a degreed theologian, but he studied and discussed theology with some of the best theologians and scholars of his day. And in my considered opinion, this association and sharing places Teilhard and Teilhardian thought in a better position than some of his critics would like to admit.

As previously stated, this volume affords the reader a privileged insight into the very core of Teilhard's soul. The Chinese exile was never easy for him. In public he was the priest-scientist, the gracious guest, and the witty conversationalist of Peking's salons. Privately he was, as his secretary and friend Father Leroy, S. J., has written, a man often in deepest anguish. The years 1942-1945 were especially difficult for Teilhard. While he was studying and conversing with Father Allegra, a terrible war raged in Europe (and in his beloved France), and his unpublished manuscripts continued to pile up on his desk. In April, 1944, he had sent a copy of *The Phenomenon of Man* to Rome for ecclesiastical approval, only to learn on August 6, 1944, that approval was again denied. I am sure that sometime during this terrible exile, Teilhard must have made his own these haunting words of Dante: "Thou shalt leave behind everything beloved most dearly; and this is the arrow which the bow of exile first shoots. Thou shalt experience how salt is the taste of another's bread, and how hard a path it is, the going up and down the stairs of others." (*Paradiso*, Canto XVII, 55-60) And yet, through the pages of this marvelous book, we know that Teilhard was never really a prisoner! If he was at times bitter, he was never broken, for he — like Paul and Ignatius and Scotus — knew Christ!

My Conversations with Teilhard de Chardin on the Primacy of Christ is, then, more than just interesting reading. It does more, too, than answer important questions and give a precious insight into Teilhard's interior life. For in this volume there is the skeletal outline for a real in-depth study of *The Divine Milieu* and Teilhardian Christology. Scholars can (with Allegra) follow Teilhard step by step through the Scriptures, the Fathers, and Franciscan thought. And then they can, if they wish — if they believe in what Teilhard called "the sacred duty of research" — not only furnish us with a fully developed Teilhardian Christology, but can go beyond Teilhardian thought itself. This last effort, I believe, is what would please Teilhard most.

Finally, a word of congratulations and thanks to Father Bernardino M. Bonansea, my brother in Christ and St. Francis, for giving this important work in Teilhardiana to the English-speaking world. Father Bonansea has done much, especially during his years at the Catholic University, to spread Scotistic thought. Now he adds to it a Teilhardian insight. Not only scholars but anyone interested in the Teilhardian or the Scotistic synthesis will profit from his arduous labors—and one would like to think that both John Duns Scotus and Pierre Teilhard de Chardin know of this. In fact, I am sure they do.

June 8, 1970

ROMANO STEPHEN ALMAGNO, O. F. M.
Librarian-bibliographer and
Member of the Board of Directors

American Teilhard de Chardin Association, Inc.
157 E. 72nd Street, New York, N. Y. 10021

CONTENTS

	Page
PREFACE	7
TRANSLATOR'S INTRODUCTION	15
AUTHOR'S INTRODUCTION	21
AUTHOR'S NOTE	33
PART ONE	37
PART TWO	55
PART THREE	83
CONCLUSION	109
TRANSLATOR'S NOTES	113

TRANSLATOR'S INTRODUCTION

In presenting this account of a series of conversations between Père Pierre Teilhard de Chardin and the Franciscan Father Allegra, it is necessary to introduce the author of the original Italian manuscript and to describe briefly the contribution the account makes to a proper understanding of the thought and personality of the renowned Jesuit scientist.

Gabriel M. Allegra, O. F. M., is president of the Franciscan Biblical Institute, which was established in 1945 in Peking, China, and transferred in 1948 to Hong Kong, where it has since been located. The primary purpose of the Institute was to translate into modern Chinese the entire Bible from the original texts in Hebrew, Aramaic, and Greek, and to provide each book with an introduction and an up-to-date commentary.

This gigantic undertaking had been the dream of Father Allegra since his seminary days in his native Sicily, and was brought to completion in 1961 with the publication of the last of the eleven volumes that include both the Old and the New Testament. The work has been hailed by Paul Cardinal Yu Pin, President of Fu-Jen Catholic University, Taipei, as the greatest scholarly achievement of the Catholic Church in China and as a turning point in its history. It has won the enthusiastic approval of many Chinese scholars and has rendered an unparalleled service to the entire Christian community. It will undoubtedly go down in history as a permanent testimony to the genius of the scholarly Franciscan priest who first conceived it and carried it to completion with the aid of coworkers in the Institute.

I have known Father Allegra since his student days at the Athenaeum Antonianum in Rome, and our friendship has continued through our years of missionary labor in China. When returning from a recent journey to Taiwan, I stopped at Hong Kong and visited my old friend, whom I had not seen for several years. The name of Teilhard de Chardin came up casually in conversation and led to Allegra's disclosure of his association with the famous Jesuit scholar. My immediate reaction to — and consequent disappointment in — the sudden discovery is described by Allegra in the introduction to his account. However, he fails to mention the surprise — or should I say shock? — that he caused me in September, 1966, when we met again at Merton College, Oxford, at the International Scotistic Congress. At that time he handed me a fifty-three page manuscript containing a detailed account of conversations with Père Teilhard which he had previously refused to write out despite my earnest request that he do so. When he handed me the manuscript, he gave me full authority to use it in any way I pleased, saying, "As far as I am concerned, I want to forget this matter completely and concentrate on the work I have at hand, the publication of the entire Chinese Bible in a single volume." This project he completed in 1968.

This is, in brief, the immediate background of Father Allegra's account, which I am privileged to present in an English version. The circumstances that led to the meeting and the subsequent conversations between the two men are related by Allegra in his introduction and do not need any further comment. However, a word must be said about the content of the account and the importance it may have for future evaluations of Père Teilhard de Chardin's thought and personality.

The theory that Christ, the Word Incarnate, holds absolute primacy in God's creative plan, so that, as St. Paul says, he is the firstborn of every creature and all things have been made for him and because of him, is perhaps the boldest and most impressive doctrine advanced by John Duns Scotus, the leader of the theological school that bears his name. This thesis constitutes the central theme of the discussions between Allegra and Teilhard de Chardin during their weekly meetings in Peking. The keen interest shown by Teilhard in Scotus' Christocentric doctrine as explained to him by Allegra is a clear indication of the many points of similarity that he found between Scotus' theory and his own view of Christ as Alpha and Omega or, to use his own expression, Christ the Pleroma.

For both Scotus and Teilhard, Christ in his divine and human nature is the center of the universe and the reason for the entire order of creation.

However, while Scotus conceives Christocentrism primarily within the supernatural order and with no direct bearing on the theory of evolution, Teilhard extends it to the order of nature and makes it an essential part of his evolutionary theory. Scotus, the theologian, arrives at his conclusion from the point of view of the logical moments, as it were, in God's creative plan. This plan, he argues, requires that God's supreme work, the Incarnation of his Son, be first and foremost in his mind. It cannot be subordinated to or conditioned by any creatural event, let alone man's revolt against God through sin. Teilhard, the scientist, arrives at his own conclusion from the study of nature and evolution or, more exactly, the phenomena, which he attempts to integrate with the data of Christian revelation, especially the teaching of St. Paul.

It is not my purpose to pass judgment on either view. However, one thing stands out very clearly, and that is the central position that Christ holds in both ideologies. Christ so dominated the thought of the Franciscan master that Christocentrism has become a chief characteristic of the Scotistic school as well as of traditional Franciscan spirituality. Teilhard de Chardin, on his part, had such a passionate love for Christ — the expression is Father Allegra's — that he not only made all his speculation converge on him, but he "Christified," as it were, the entire universe. In so doing he went a step further than Scotus, whose view he wholeheartedly endorsed, and ventured into an area full of theological implications, as the present account indicates. No matter what stand one may wish to take on Teilhard's vision—for such is what it appeared to him to be—it must be said that he rendered an invaluable service to theology by popularizing the Christocentric doctrine and hence, at least indirectly, the idea of Christ's absolute primacy championed by Scotus and the Scotistic school.

Father Allegra's report of conversations with Père Teilhard over a period of three years is a most fitting introduction to the thought of the renowned French Jesuit. It reveals both the content of Teilhard's message to the world and the motive and spirit that animate it. Writing from the vantage point of personal friendship, Allegra describes the problems and anxieties that beset Teilhard during his most trying years and brings forth many interesting traits of his complex and fascinating personality.

A sincere admirer of Teilhard's genius, Allegra attempts to penetrate his far-sighted and challenging views, but at the same time he does not fail to point out, whenever necessary, the apparent conflict between his doctrines and traditional Catholic teaching. Teilhard's reaction is usually as frank as the remarks of his friend and critic, and from this clash of minds arises a lively discussion between two learned yet unaffected men whose only concern is to ascertain truth. This Allegra has tried faithfully to reproduce in the pages that follow. His account, it is hoped, will prove helpful to those who are genuinely interested in Teilhard de Chardin's thought and its dominant theme: Christ, Alpha and Omega, Christ the Pleroma.

The Catholic University of America
Washington, D. C.

BERNARDINO M. BONANSEA, O. F. M.

AUTHOR'S INTRODUCTION

One day in Peking, toward the end of April, 1942, I received a telephone call from Archbishop Mario Zanin, Apostolic Delegate to China. He asked me to go to his office, as he had something to discuss with me. When I went to Nai-Tse-Fu, the Apostolic Delegate's residence, a conversation took place between the archbishop and me which I wish to report here in substance, for it reveals the mingled feelings of affection, admiration, and apprehension of which Père Teilhard was then the object.

Archbishop Zanin. Do you know Père Teilhard de Chardin?

Father Gabriel Allegra. Yes, Excellency, I met him several times, first at Kobe in Japan, and later at the French Embassy, at St. Michael's Church, and the Institute of Hautes Etudes in Tientsin.

Zanin. Well, then, I would like to give this devout priest and renowned scientist the satisfaction of seeing one of his works published. It is a work that is most dear to him, for he rates it over and above all his other works, either scientific, philosophical, or religious. The censors of his Society have refused to give him a nihil obstat. I ask you to read the work and see whether it is possible, in the spirit of St. Francis, a saint so dear to Père Teilhard, to comply with his and my own request. However, if you really think that either because of its doctrinal content or for other reasons the work cannot be approved, I would ask you to put your objections in writing.

I tried to decline the task, and to this effect I mentioned the names of certain learned priests whom I considered to be better qualified as censors than me. However, the archbishop was immovable. He opened his desk drawer and took out a typewritten manuscript which he handed to me. I noticed that the paper of the single-spaced manuscript was of a very poor quality and the pages had almost turned yellow. The manuscript carried the title: *Le milieu divin*. On the front inside page the following dedication was written:

> *"Sic Deus dilexit mundum"* —
> *"A ceux qui aiment le monde*
> *cette esquisse d'un Optimisme chrétien"*

That is, "God so loved the world . . ." (John 3:16). "To those who love the world, this essay on Christian Optimism."

The manuscript immediately aroused my curiosity. I began to page through it and, while still listening to the Apostolic Delegate, I turned to the last page and noticed with some surprise the place and date of the manuscript's composition: *Tientsin, November 1926 — March 1927*. Almost instinctively, I interrupted the archbishop and said: "Excellency, this is a very old work. How is it that

AUTHOR'S INTRODUCTION

Père Teilhard wishes to have it published now, fifteen years after it was written?" In answer to my question the Apostolic Delegate gave me complete information concerning the case of Père Teilhard, with the evident intention of persuading me to be an extremely indulgent censor.

After I returned to the Franciscan house in Ly Kwang Kiao, Peking, I began to read the manuscript and to make notes on anything that appeared to me as new, shocking, daring, or even wrong. At the end of this delicate task, I wrote my report as censor, which turned out to be negative. (If the archives of the Apostolic Delegation to China have been preserved, the report should still be there.) As the principal reasons for my refusal to approve the work I mentioned its ambiguous terminology and a confusion between the natural and supernatural orders. Moreover, I felt that throughout the work the reality and the meaning of sin were not given sufficient consideration, and that thus the redemptive value of the sacrifice of the Cross was understated. Finally, I thought that its concept of the Redemption did not correspond with the teaching of revelation taken as a whole.

Yet, while pointing out the reasons for my objection to the work, I could not fail to bring forth also those points which had literally fascinated me: the powerful synthesis, the absolute primacy and finality of Christ, the Christian Church as the gravitational center of man's ascent to Christ, and the consecration of the world in Christ. I concluded my report as censor by saying that perhaps few readers would understand Teilhard de Chardin's thought, while many others, for lack of adequate training, would be led into error by his daring ideas. Hence I could not in conscience grant the nihil obstat. [NOTE: *Le milieu divin*, like all the other major works by Teilhard de Chardin, was published posthumously by the Editions du Seuil (Paris, 1957), and without the nihil obstat. The English translation appeared in Great Britain under the title *Le Milieu Divin* (London: Collins, 1960), and in the United States of America under the title *The Divine Milieu* (New York: Harper and Row, 1960).]

The archbishop seemed to be pleased with my report and told me that other censors too — he mentioned a few names — had expressed more or less the same view. He then gave me an order that took me by surprise and caused me a great deal of embarrassment: "Now go and tell Père Teilhard what you have told me. He already knows and is quite pleased that a Franciscan has been chosen as the definitive censor of his work.... I assure you that your meeting will be a pleasant one and you will both be satisfied."

I waited for two days. Then, on a memorable Sunday toward the end of May, 1942, after celebrating Mass in the chapel of the Italian Embassy, I picked up the famous manuscript, put it into my briefcase together with a copy of my report as censor, and went straight to Rue Labrousse, in the former diplomatic legations' quarter, where Père Teilhard was residing. He received me at once in his office on the ground floor, and our meeting lasted two hours. As things turned out, this was to be only the first of our meetings, for, as I was leaving, he said repeatedly: "Father, I will be waiting for you. On Sunday at this time I am always free, and I am very anxious to see you again." That marked the beginning of our weekly conversations. They went on almost without interruption until 1945 and left me with many indelible memories.

For a better understanding of the kind of impressions I received from my conversations with Père Teilhard, a few observations are in order. First of all, I was impressed by the humility he showed in listening with sincere good will to the remarks of either a philosophical or a theological nature that I took the liberty to make on his thought. He often said to me: *"Moi, je ne fais pas de la philosophie ni de la théologie; j'étudie le phénomène"* (I speak neither as a philosopher nor as a theologian; I study the phenomenon). When I pointed out that for him, as for the ancient Greek sages, natural science is inseparable from theology and philosophy, he would agree and say: "That is right, but I study primarily the phenomenon."[1]

I could not help admiring him as he discussed such scientific issues as the expansion of the universe, cephalization, the biosphere, the noosphere, the convergent ascent of the spirit, the sacredness of the earth, the seat of the noosphere and yet so extremely small when compared to the gigantic galaxies. However, what impressed and touched me most deeply was his explanation or, rather, explanations, for he would return to the subject over and over again, of Christ as Alpha and Omega, of Christ the Pleroma.

During one of our first meetings I said: "Père Teilhard" — the conversations were carried out in French — "all you are saying, if we leave aside the scientific arguments which are beyond my competence, is part of the traditional teaching of the Franciscan school. It represents the great contribution that the Venerable John Duns Scotus has made to Christian thought." I did my best to explain to him the substance of the teaching of the Subtle Doctor — this is the title by which Scotus is known — and then I concluded: "I am of the opinion that both St. Paul and St. John can or perhaps must be interpreted in this sense." I noticed immediately the profound emotion that my words had caused in him, an emotion that manifested itself in an unusual sparkling of his extremely dark eyes. Our souls were vibrating. He rose from his chair and embraced me most affectionately, bending toward me because he was so tall. In so doing he said: "I will be waiting for you next Sunday. Be sure to bring with you the New Testament in Greek and the texts of Scotus. We shall read them together."

In several of our subsequent meetings we read together the texts of St. Paul and Scotus and commented upon them. Once I remarked to Père Teilhard: "It seems to me that what the Church needs today is a cosmic theology, a theology to be worked out in the light of the universal and absolute primacy of Christ." Père Teilhard agreed and said: *"Oui, c'est le mot; il nous faut une théologie cosmique, ce sera la théologie de l'avenir"* (Yes, that is the word; we need a cosmic theology, and that will be the theology of the future). Later he came back to this same idea time and again, and on several occasions he exhorted me to work for this purpose.[2]

To mention some other features of our conversations, it is worth noting that we never discussed politics or war, even though our meetings were held between 1942 and 1945, when China and the whole world were at war. We seldom talked about our superiors or confreres, and when we did so, Père Teilhard always showed great understanding and charity. He liked my frankness and sincerity, which I defined from our very first meeting as the Pauline *parresia*. I am sure he would agree with me when I say — even though this is many years after his death — that he knew little Scholastic philosophy, had a natural dislike for metaphysics, and was close to Maurice Blondel in his philosophical thinking. While lacking the knowledge of many learned professors, he nourished himself on certain basic ideas or *idées-lumière*, as he used to call them, of St. Augustine, whose thought he knew very well, and drew heavily from the teaching of St. Paul, whom he used to read in the original Greek. As he came upon certain great new ideas or the ideas of some great minds, he immediately tried to fit them into his own personal synthesis and draw from them an abundant and unsuspected richness. It was then necessary to let him talk, for he was irresistible. In brief, Père Teilhard had an intuitive mind and was a mystic who was absorbed in his interior world and completely possessed by it. Because of his mystical cast of mind, it was practically impossible to go astray in conversing with him, even when the subject of our conversation would bear on different and apparently unrelated topics. He would make everything converge on his chief ideas of Christ as Alpha and Omega, Christ the Pleroma, the sacredness of nature and matter, the universe as the royal mantle of Christ.[3]

Since the death of Père Teilhard I have been repeatedly asked by several of my friends to write out and publish the substance of my conversations with him as a memorial to this renowned scientist. I always refused to do so. The last pressing invitation came to me from my confrere Father Bernardino Bonansea, professor of philosophy at the Catholic University of America in Washington, D. C., when he called on me in September, 1965. But to him too I said "no," even though my refusal caused no little disappointment to one who has been a close friend of mine since the days of our college studies in Rome. However, this year, on the occasion of the seventh centenary of the birth of the Venerable John Duns Scotus, patron of our Biblical Institute in Hong Kong, the Very Reverend Charles Balić, O. F. M., president of the Commission for the critical edition of Scotus' works, has put so much pressure on me that he has overcome my disinclination to put the substance of these conversations into writing, and I have finally given in.

But how should I present the thought of Père Teilhard, even if I reduce it to a single theme, as I have proposed to do? A scholarly report seems out of question; it would be extremely boring. As I was pondering the matter, all of a sudden the idea dawned on me that a report in the form of a dialogue like the dialogues of Plato, Cicero, Galileo, Tasso, Manzoni, and many Fathers of the Church would perhaps serve the purpose. At first the idea frightened me, but later I took comfort in the fact that a similar project had been carried out successfully by Jean Guitton,[4] who only recently had presented us with an extremely interesting dialogue on the thought and spirituality of Père Pouget, C. M.[5] I decided therefore on the dialogue form, and at the same time I proposed to limit myself chiefly and almost exclusively to the theme of the primacy of Christ, not without adding here and there some hints and observations that might help toward a better understanding of the main theme. My decision was not an arbitrary one. In fact, the discussion during those happy hours which were for Père Teilhard a time for intellectual relaxation —

he used to speak of *détente spirituelle*—was centered almost entirely on "the Great Christ," even though occasionally we would turn our conversation to Pascal, St. Francis of Assisi, the Scholastics, Chinese philosophy, and Dante Alighieri. In this connection I may point out that because of his close friendship with his confrere Père Auguste Valensin, a renowned Dante scholar,[6] Père Teilhard had a great love for Dante, even though he never set aside time to make a special study of him. A characteristic feature of our conversations, it is worth mentioning, consisted in reading the texts of the New Testament in the original Greek, a language with which Père Teilhard was familiar, notwithstanding his assertion that he had forgotten it. The Latin texts of Scotus, which Father asked me to read, translate, and comment upon, were taken almost exclusively from the *Summula Scotistica* of Father Diomede Scaramuzzi,[7] and occasionally from the *Doctrina philosophica et theologica* of Father Parthenius Minges.[8]

I have divided the present dialogue into three parts, and in it I have earnestly tried to reproduce, if not the exact words, which would be impossible, at least the real and genuine meaning of our conversations at Rue Labrousse. As for certain particular statements, I feel even today sounding in my ears not only Père Teilhard's French expressions but also the very inflections of his voice, just as at the time of my writing I had the vivid impression of seeing him face to face and of staring at the sparkling of his eyes. Some readers will no doubt notice how lively and stimulating our conversations were, but no one will be able to fully understand the jovial and friendly fashion in which they were carried out unless he has known Père Teilhard personally.

One last recollection. At one time, long before his departure, Père Teilhard told me about an extended visit he would make in Tientsin. He then presented me with the typescript of *Le milieu divin* and a short but valuable essay, *La parole attendue*. On the frontispiece of *Le milieu divin* he wrote the following dedication:

> *"Au R. P. Allegra*
> *en grande sympathie*
> *in X ... Ω.*
> *Teilhard de Chardin"*

That is, "To the Reverend Father Allegra, with great affection, in Christ ... Omega. Teilhard de Chardin."

He went on to explain how Christ is the Omega point and spoke with such eloquence and enthusiasm that it was a real pleasure to listen to him. After a little while I said to him: "Père Teilhard, what you are saying is, without your being aware of it, a concept that has already been expressed by Duns Scotus in what may be called *Elevatio mentis in Deum:* "You are infinitely good, communicating the rays of your goodness most liberally; to you, the most lovable, all things tend, each in its own way, as to their ultimate end."[9] Père Teilhard was delighted. He rose from his chair, took me to his office, and there he went out of his way to explain to me a large diagram of the "Tree of Life." The tree was dominated by the figure of a man illuminated by a flash of light coming from above. This was supposed to represent the mystery of the Incarnation by which God — Père Teilhard explained — *"non minuit naturam sed sacravit"* (did not lessen nature but made it sacred). Thereupon he began to talk with loving tenderness about the Blessed Mother, Mary Immaculate, who, according to his theory of orthogenesis, fulfills the unique and glorious task of sublimating mankind or, as Dante puts it, of ennobling human nature.

"We must talk again about this subject when I come back from Tientsin," said Père Teilhard.

"Of course," I replied.

And talk we did. What follows is a free but accurate record of what we said in those memorable days about the absolute primacy of Christ, while a furious war raged like a wild hurricane over the entire planet.

Hong Kong, 1966

GABRIEL M. ALLEGRA, O. F. M.

Author's Note

Although I agree with many writers that a dialogue should contain no footnotes by the author, yet because of the widespread reputation of Père Teilhard de Chardin and the consequent need of shedding light on both the man and his thought with factual data, I consider it necessary to call the reader's attention to the following points:

I. The principal works consulted by this writer on the subject of his Peking conversations with Père Teilhard are:

   Diomede Scaramuzzi, *Duns Scoto: Summula*. Edizioni "Testi cristiani." Florence: Libreria Editrice Fiorentina, 1932.

   Parthenius Minges, *Ioannis Duns Scoti doctrina philosophica et theologica*. 2 vols. Quaracchi: Typographia Collegii S. Bonaventurae, 1930.

   Ludovico Ciganotto, *Saggi di critica interna sul trattato "De primo principio" del B. Giovanni Duns Scoto*. Gemona: Toso, 1926.

   Leonardo M. Bello, "Litterae encyclicae de universali Christi primatu atque regalitate," *Acta Ordinis Fratrum Minorum*, LII (1933), 293-311.

   Chrysostome Urrubéhéty, *Christus, Alpha et Omega, seu de Christi universali regno*. 2nd ed. Lille: Girard, 1910.

II. In the exposition of the Christocentric doctrine and Christ's Redemption out of pure love, I availed myself, but without compromising the truth of our conversations, of Efrem Bettoni's article, "Il primato di Cristo e i suoi riflessi nella dottrina ascetica francescana," *Quaderni di spiritualità francescana*, XII (1966), 38-51.

AUTHOR'S NOTE

III. The persons, places, and episodes referred to in the course of the dialogue are all real.

IV. As far as the present writer is concerned, he knows of only two persons who during the pontificate of Pope Pius XII invoked and almost prophesied the Ecumenical Council: Père Teilhard de Chardin and Egidio Cardinal Vagnozzi, formerly Apostolic Delegate to the United States of America.

V. The typescript of *Le milieu divin*, here and there annotated by both Père Teilhard and myself, is in the present writer's keeping, together with Teilhard's short note *Sur la notion de la perfection chrétienne* and his message *La parole attendue*.[10]

MY CONVERSATIONS
WITH
TEILHARD DE CHARDIN
ON THE
PRIMACY OF CHRIST

PART ONE

Teilhard. I was waiting for you. Please take a seat, and let us begin immediately with the discussion of our theme, which I would like to formulate in the following terms: the universe is ordered to Christ; it is the Pleroma of Christ. You have told me that these statements contain a great and sublime truth, but that you do not quite agree with their formulation. I want to emphasize once more that I am not speaking as a theologian or a philosopher; I am only concerned with those who *foris sunt* (are outside), the scientists. St. Francis Xavier, as you know, had his Indies to evangelize; well, my Indies are the field of modern scientists. What an immense multitude of souls in search of God; if only someone would come to their aid and show the way to him (*"quaerunt Deum, si forte attrectent eum"* — cf. Acts 17:27). I feel as if I hear their anguished appeal: *"Transi et adiuva nos"* (Come and help us — cf. Acts 16:9). Up to this point I see clearly my mission, but I am not a theologian and therefore I sincerely appreciate the opportunity to listen to a theologian who will confirm me in my conviction and my passionate love for *le Grand Christ* (the Great Christ).

Allegra. Father, I am sorry to say that you do not have before you a theologian but, rather, a humble son of St. Francis of Assisi, who, like you, is fascinated by the cosmic greatness of Christ — *Rex totius universitatis* (King of the whole universe) — which is but the logical consequence of the doctrine of the Franciscan school, and especially of John Duns Scotus, the great theologian of the absolute and universal primacy of Christ. Like him, I can hardly understand how one can speak of the Incarnate Word as the greatest, the most sublime, and the holiest of all beings, and at the same time maintain that he was "occasioned" by sin.

As I have told you before, I was deeply impressed by your statement: *"Le Christ évangélique, imaginé et aimé aux dimensions d'un monde méditerranéen"* (The Christ of the gospels, conceived and loved according to the dimensions of a Mediterranean world). That statement made me think that from certain points of view the entire missionary endeavor may appear to be a failure. Yet my persistent optimism remains unshaken because of the two fundamental doctrines of creation and Incarnation or, to be more specific, of the doctrine of the Incarnate Word *"per quem omnia facta sunt et in quo omnia constant"* (through whom all things have been made and in whom all things hold together — cf. Col. 1:16-17). Perhaps you will find it strange, but nevertheless you may be pleased to know that a famous Italian jurist, His Excellency Alberto De Stefani, when speaking with me of the sad and disruptive effects of this cruel war, concluded his discussion with the following words: "After all, we must always remain hopeful, both because we believe in creation, that is, in a creative God, and because we believe in the mystery of the Incarnation."

Teilhard. This is a most impressive and truthful statement. Please go on and speak to me with this same candor and Franciscan kindness. See, Father Allegra, even though I have started from different premises, the premises of science, I have nevertheless reached the same conclusions as you. The only point of disagreement is that I express my thought with a different vocabulary. As I told you before, I try to make myself understood by the men of today, who frown at the very thought of the hylomorphic theory or any other Aristotelian or Scholastic doctrine. You have criticized the ambiguity of my vocabulary, and no doubt you have done so for good reasons. Yet it is the precise purpose I intend to achieve that, as it were, compels me to use such a vocabulary.

To get back to the theme of "the Great Christ," I know from my conversations with d'Alès, [11] de Grandmaison,[12] Lebreton[13] — I am sure these names are familiar to you — that along with the theory of the Word become Incarnate almost exclusively for the Redemption of man, there is also the Franciscan doctrine of an Incarnation independent of sin. Unfortunately, my type of work does not allow me to devote myself to the study of this fascinating subject. However, St. Paul, both through his doctrine of the Pleroma and in his epistles to the Colossians and the Ephesians, teaches me and makes me realize how true it is that Christ is the Alpha and the Omega, the center and the end of the entire universe. Please tell me: how is this doctrine received today in theological circles? Does it have any followers, or is it perhaps treated as a merely academic issue, if not completely neglected?

Allegra. Father, rather than being neglected, this doctrine is either attacked by the ordinary manualists of dogmatic theology or, what is worse, treated with that kind of condescending pity which really hurts.

Teilhard. Oh, les professeurs! Il y en a des myopes! (Oh, the professors! How short-sighted many of them are!)

Allegra. In the more serious and profound theological works the doctrine is usually presented alongside and compared with the commonly accepted theory that the Incarnation is for Redemption. There are also those who, following in the footsteps of Suárez, attempt to reconcile the two seemingly conflicting doctrines.[14] In my opinion, a clear and scholarly exposition of the entire issue is to be found in Michel's article in the *Dictionnaire de théologie catholique.*[15] But if I am not mistaken, the Franciscans have been left almost alone in their defense of the absolute primacy of Christ, or the doctrine that the Incarnation has not been occasioned by sin. Some years ago our former Minister General, the Most Reverend Leonard M. Bello, O. F. M., issued a letter to the Order of Friars Minor in which he expounded this beautiful doctrine and made an earnest appeal to his friars to teach, spread, and defend it.[16] In a well-documented presentation, Father Bello shows that, along with the teaching of theological manuals, there have always been in the Church, as there are today, great thinkers, mystics, and saints who accept and defend Christ's kingship or absolute primacy. It is gratifying to see that even some Anglican exegetes, such as the renowned Westcott,[17] wholeheartedly support this same doctrine and base their teaching on the Scriptures, especially the letters of St. Paul.

Teilhard. Tell me more about the Church Doctors and defenders of this doctrine, even though for me, who have no time to do much reading, the teaching of St. Paul is more than sufficient. If I well recall, Bishop d'Herbigny told me some years ago that even the Russians and the Orthodox in general believe in this doctrine.[18]

Allegra. Père Teilhard, as far as the theologians, or rather the Orthodox Fathers, are concerned, here is what I can tell you from the documentation of Father Bello's letter. Because of their theory of the divinization of humanity through the

Incarnation, they either explicitly or implicitly subordinate the Redemption to the Incarnation. It is this latter, in effect, that glorifies God in a special way and divinizes the cosmos. The Orthodox Archbishop of Peking, the Most Reverend Victor, and his theologian, Professor Zeiseff, are not acquainted with Western theology, but they know that on this point the Franciscan school is close to their teaching, and — so they told me — they feel very proud of it. The same idea has repeatedly been expressed to me by Signora Varaschini, a very learned and devout Russian lady who is a convert from the Orthodox Church to Catholicism.

As for the thought of the Fathers of the Church, I can point to the findings of one of my French confreres, Père Chrysostome Urrutibéhéty — I think the name is Basque — who, in his work *Christus, Alpha et Omega,* analyzes the opinion of the Greek and Latin Fathers up to the Scholastic revival of the sixteenth and seventeenth centuries.[19] Except for some minor inaccuracies of historical criticism, the work as a whole gives the reader the definite impression that the doctrine of the absolute primacy of Christ is by no means so strange and extreme as the ordinary manuals of dogmatic theology seem to indicate. On the contrary, the doctrine is deeply rooted in the great tradition of the ancient Church. It has been held by such authoritative Fathers as St. Irenaeus, St. Athanasius, St. John

Chrysostom, St. Cyril of Alexandria, Anastasius of Sinai, and Isaac of Nineveh, to mention only a few names.[20] Yet, in my opinion, many of these famous witnesses to Tradition — and I include among them the greatest of all, St. Augustine — did not attempt to make a synthesis of the doctrine of the Incarnation independent of sin and the doctrine of redemptive Incarnation. The only exception is the attempt made in this direction by the powerful mind of Rupert of Deutz.[21]

Unfortunately, after Rupert it became the custom to propose the doctrine of the absolute primacy of Christ not as a revealed truth but merely as a hypothesis: If Adam had not sinned, would the Word have become incarnate? To such a question the great leaders of Scholasticism, St. Thomas Aquinas and St. Bonaventure, answered in the negative, and in so doing they went against their respective masters, St. Albert the Great and Alexander of Hales. However, it must be said to their credit that both Schoolmen held to certain doctrinal principles which, if carried to their logical conclusions, might lead to the doctrine of absolute primacy. Perhaps the motives behind their theory, as well as the motives behind St. Augustine's view, were, first, fear of taking a stand that would seem to run against many explicit statements of Scripture; secondly, the much simpler view that presents the doctrine of the Incarnation as ordered uniquely, or at least principally, to Redemption; and, finally, the senti-

43

ments of piety and devotion that such a doctrine immediately arouses in the hearts of the faithful. Now, if one reflects for a moment on the influence that the teaching of those Doctors, especially St. Thomas Aquinas, has exerted upon Catholic schools, it is hardly to be expected that the doctrine of Christ's absolute primacy would receive from the manualists the consideration it deserves. Often their treatment gives the impression that they do not even suspect that the question at issue is not merely one of devotion, but one that concerns the greatest glory of Christ and most probably—to me, it is certain—a datum of revelation to be found both in Sacred Scripture and in the Fathers and Doctors of the Church.

Teilhard. Père Allegra, you are no doubt acquainted with the case of Galileo. How many in those days—and they were not all Catholics—refused even to discuss the affirmations of that genius and look at the heavens through his telescope because that probing instrument and that vision would have overthrown the Ptolemaic-Aristotelian system of astronomy. Intellectual sloth and exaggerated conservatism in the field of science, of all the sciences, are often an obstacle to progress, until a real thinker arises who sees intuitively, as in a flash, the whole truth and presents its elements in a harmonious synthesis. Sorry to have interrupted you; please go ahead and tell me more about the Pleroma of Christ.

Allegra. Père Teilhard, I prefer not to speak of Pleroma in the sense you attach to this word, since the term has in St. Paul a variety of meanings and may lend itself to ambiguity. I would rather use the expression "the absolute primacy of Christ" or "the universal kingship of Christ." To resume the thread of our discourse, I would like to call your attention to the fact that, although this doctrine is disregarded by most manuals of theology, it continues to fascinate a great number of brilliant Church scholars. I do not think it is necessary to mention here all the representatives of the Franciscan school who without exception on this point follow their leader, John Duns Scotus. But I cannot fail to bring forth the names of some of the principal figures in the past, such as St. Bernardine of Siena[22] and St. Lawrence of Brindisi,[23] and a selected group of learned and devout theologians in more recent and present times. Among the latter there are many Frenchmen, such as Père Déodat de Basly,[24] Père Chrysostom, previously mentioned, Père Valentin Marie Breton,[25] P. Marie Bonaventure,[26] P. Jean F. Bonnefoy,[27] P. Jean-Marie Bissen,[28] the Canadian P. Ephrem Longpré,[29] the Croatian Father Charles Balić, president of the Commission for the critical edition of Scotus' works,[30] the Rector of Sacred Heart University in Milan, Father Agostino Gemelli,[31] and many others. Among the defenders of the doctrine outside the Franciscan Order

I would like to mention Pierre Cardinal de Bérulle,[32] the Venerable Jean Jacques Olier,[33] Bishop Bougaud,[34] Bishop Bonomelli,[35] Father Frederick W. Faber,[36] Bishop Westcott, the Anglican exegete already mentioned,[37] and, if I properly understand his thought, the great theologian Matthias Scheeben,[38] the Italian philosopher Carmelo Ottaviano,[39] and above all St. Francis de Sales.[40]

Teilhard. Father, you have mentioned many names, but three among them are particularly interesting to me: Scotus, St. Francis de Sales, and Gemelli, for whom I have a special admiration. I would like to know more about them.

Allegra. Père Teilhard, as far as Scotus is concerned, the next time we meet I will bring a short poem by your English confrere Gerard Manley Hopkins, entitled "Duns Scotus' Oxford," which Madame de Margerie has found in the library of the *Alliance Française* and has kindly copied out for me in her own handwriting.[41] I am sure you will like it, and it will offer us the opportunity to talk again about the Knight of the Immaculate Conception, as Scotus is called. St. Francis de Sales expounds his thought in his treatise *On the Love of God* in terms that make palatable to the reader—to use an English expression—those texts of Scotus which seem to present a special difficulty for the average person.[42] Father Gemelli does not engage in any discussions: he simply presents his thought with vigor and earnestness. He gives me the impression that he has read a lot but has reflected even more on the subject of the absolute primacy of Christ. To be perfectly honest, I must say that I feel about him exactly as I feel about you. He seems to grasp this doctrine by some sort of intuition in reading St. Paul and St. John. He strives to feel Christ as St. Francis did, and he defends Christ's absolute primacy with the arguments of Scotus.[43]

Perhaps you will be surprised at my mention of another name that I withheld a little while ago, the name of Don Luigi Sturzo.[44] This most sincere and devout priest, an internationally known sociologist, is also an enthusiastic defender of the doctrine of the absolute primacy of Christ.[45]

Teilhard. To tell you the truth, I am not altogether surprised, for all the sciences, like all beings, demand a principle, a center, and an end, the Alpha and Omega, and that can only be Christ, the Incarnate Word, "le Grand Christ" *in quo omnia constant* (the Great Christ, in whom all things hold together — cf. Col. 1:17). But I cannot deny the fact that I am most pleased to hear that Father Gemelli and Don Sturzo think this way. Now tell me about Scotus' thought. Have you brought his texts?

Allegra. I have brought with me Father Scaramuzzi's *Summula Scotistica* and the New Testament in Greek, just as you wished me to do.

Teilhard. May I ask you, then, to summarize for me as clearly as possible *cette grande doctrine* (this great doctrine). Next time we shall read the texts, and you will explain them to me.

Allegra. Father, that is not an easy task, but I will try. Sacred Scripture teaches the absolute primacy of Christ, just as it teaches that there is another end for the Incarnation, namely, the Redemption of mankind. The Fathers of the Church have affirmed both the primacy and the Redemption without attempting their synthesis, that is, without coordinating in a harmonious system the two doctrines or, as you would say, the whole truth. St. Thomas and St. Bonaventure have taught that the primary end of the Incarnation is Redemption, and their authority, especially that of St. Thomas, has led to the almost official recognition of such a doctrine. John Duns Scotus took a stand against the two great masters, just as he had done in regard to the doctrine of the Immaculate Conception of Mary, and attempted a synthesis of the two doctrines of Christ's absolute primacy and of his Redemption. In my opinion none of Scotus' followers has added anything really new to the arguments advanced by him, although I am quite willing to admit that the French school of spirituality has drawn the extreme consequences of Scotus' incisive phrase, *"Deus voluit ab alio summe diligi"* (God willed to be loved by another in a supreme degree),[46] just as St. Francis de Sales had drawn the final consequences of Scotus' other principle, *"Deus est formaliter charitas"* (God is love by his very nature).[47]

If I am not mistaken, Père Marie Bonaventure's meditations on the Blessed Sacrament and some of the spiritual reflections of the Venerable Olier, Gay, and Faber, to mention only a few names,[48] are also based on Scotistic doctrine. This is especially true in the case of the main trend of the Franciscan school in the sixteenth and seventeenth centuries, according to which even the sacramental presence of Christ in the Eucharist and the Immaculate Conception have been willed by God, *the First Love,* without reference to sin. Surprisingly enough, this teaching finds its confirmation in some of the writings of the Church Fathers and mystics.

I am convinced, my dear Père Teilhard, that "sacred theology" today ought to attempt the synthesis I have just mentioned and perhaps integrate it with your own doctrine. This requires, of course, powerful minds and hearts fully inspired by the love of God, who alone can raise up such persons in his Church. My ignorance makes me say foolish things, but I do not think I am too far from the truth when I say that the so-called philosophy of science has not yet been integrated, as far as I know, into common theological doctrine. I have opened my heart to you on ·this matter, and I have shown to you in writing what have been my reactions to your work *Le milieu divin*. As you explained to me your notion of hyperphysics and of the Omega point, I reflected on it and came to the conclusion that this vigorous new trend of thought can really contribute to the renewal of Christian theology and give it new vitality.

In the Middle Ages sacred theology had a great appeal to the faithful; today I am afraid it puts even our seminarians to sleep. There must be a reason for this unfortunate situation. I think that our sacred patrimony lacks dynamism and is altogether static. Perhaps this is due to the fact that theology is cut off from the philosophy of science, which is in continuous progress and evolution. It may also be because theology is anatomized, as it were, into too many different sectors of specialization, or because it is considered more as a legacy to be preserved than as an evangelical talent to be used and developed. To give new and fresh vitality to our theology we need, in Dante's words, *"fuochi tutti contemplanti, cuori saldi, cupidi ingegni"* (men of contemplation, steadfast hearts, and eager minds — *Paradiso*, XXII, 46, 51), that is, souls that are yearning for the "Bread of Heaven" and *"i dolcissimi veri"* (the sweetest truths), as the great poet used to call science. Briefly, we need someone, or perhaps many who, like Pascal, are both men of science and great thinkers. But are we not asking too much of most of our theologians today?

Teilhard. I must interrupt you. Your last question is very serious and one that is not easy to answer. I think, however, that by organizing the work *en équipe* (as by a team) the job can be done. Your reference to Dante and Pascal is very pertinent. As far as Pascal is concerned, you will agree that a Catholic priest and French citizen like me ought to know him almost as a matter of duty; as for Dante, my good friend and confrere Père Valensin[49] has done much to make me appreciate and admire him, even though, on account of certain other pressing activities, I have never had the opportunity to study him profoundly. Yes, I fully agree with you that what the Church needs today is a theological synthesis, a cosmic theology. We must stop imposing on *le Grand Christ* our Mediterranean dimensions.

Allegra. Père Teilhard, your unsuspected admiration for Dante reminds me of a remarkable intuition of that great genius. May I be permitted to make a digression?

Teilhard. Certainly, I will be only too glad to listen to you.

Allegra. In the sun's heaven the poet sees two circles of spirits whom he describes as being like flames that dance and sing. The first circle is headed by St. Thomas and the second by St. Bonaventure. Both of these circles of "great doctors" include certain minor figures, among whom two are particularly striking, a thinker and a prophet, whom the official thirteenth-century theology masters would never have suspected of having achieved such a glory in the everlasting meadows of paradise. In St. Thomas' circle there is *"la luce eterna di Sigieri"* (the eternal light of Siger of Brabant—*Paradiso*, X, 136), while in St. Bonaventure's circle there is *"il calavrese abate Gioacchino di spirito profetico dotato"* (the prophetically endowed Abbot Joachim of Calabria—*Paradiso*, XII, 140-141). St. Thomas had fought against the first of these two doctors, and St. Bonaventure against the second. This is a most significant fact, for it shows the magnanimity of Dante's heart. But there is more to it. Dante foretells, and expresses the desire for, the emergence of a third school of thought that will make a synthesis of the two preceding ones, namely, the Dominican and the Franciscan. This school he envisions and describes as a third circle:

> And behold! a light of equal brightness
>   shone around what was there
>   like a horizon growing bright,
> and, as in early evening, stars
>   appear faintly in the sky,
>   so that their sight seems real
>   and not real,
> so I seemed to see new substances
>   making a circle outside
>   of the other two circumferences.

> O true sparkling of the Holy Spirit,
>   how suddenly glowing it became
>   to my eyes which, overcome,
>   endured it not!
>
> (*Paradiso*, XIV, 67-77)[50]

I do not know what your friend Père Valensin thinks of this, but I believe with many renowned Dante scholars that this third circle is like a symbol and a forewarning of a more comprehensive theology, a cosmic theology, as I would call it today, which would fuse and harmonize into a synthesis the thought of Plato and Aristotle, the speculation of the Arabs and all other peoples outside the Greek and Roman worlds, and the prophetic visions of the saints, such as those of Abbot Joachim.

Teilhard. Father, how true and beautiful all this is! Oh, the great heart of Dante! I cannot tell you what Père Valensin thinks of this particular subject, but I remember his telling me at one time that Dante's kindness of heart was even greater than his titanic genius.

Well, it is late today. I hope to see you next Sunday. Do not forget to bring along with you the New Testament in Greek and the writings of John Duns Scotus, as well as the little poem of Gerard Manley Hopkins. Let us go to the next room now. I want to fulfill my promise and explain to you the zone that the primates, the anthropoids, and the hominoids occupy in the "Tree of Life." That is theology, too, isn't it?

Allegra. I see in it the mystery of the Creator, and so I feel that somehow or other we are dealing with theology. The finalistic evolution, which, if I am not wrong, you also call orthogenesis, is ordered to the glory of the "Great Christ." What else, then, could that be but theology? I am convinced, my dear Père Teilhard, that this intuition of yours is an everlasting contribution to Christian theologians and philosophers, provided they are *"fuochi tutti contemplanti"* (all contemplating flames) and have *"il cuor saldo"* (a steadfast heart).

PART TWO

Teilhard. Thank you for being so punctual; kindness is the flower of charity.

Allegra. May I be allowed, Father, to give you a definition of kindness that perhaps is even more meaningful, the definition of St. Francis?

Teilhard. Please! St. Francis is so dear and so close to me! I believe he assists me in my difficulties and blesses my work. In him one can feel the presence of God the Father and the refreshing perfume of the house of Nazareth. Please tell me the definition of the lovable Poverello.

Allegra. "*Curialitas est una ex perfectionibus Dei*": Kindness is one of the perfections of God.[51]

Teilhard. That is truly a lovely definition and by far better than the usual one I have given you. I want to take it down in my notebook. [Père Teilhard writes the definition in his notebook and then he continues.] Now, moved by this courtesy, let us both talk about the "loving and lovable" Christ.

Allegra. In our previous conversations you have several times advanced the theory, which for you is more than probable, that life, including its greatest manifestation, the noosphere, may exist on some other planets. Is that correct?

Teilhard. That is absolutely right, but I do not see how your question has anything to do with the *Pleroma tou Christou* — pardon! with the absolute primacy of Christ.

Allegra. Yes, the two issues are related to each other, and their relationship is much more profound than I had thought before. The subject has been raised by the Ambassadress, Madame de Margerie, at the last reception at the French Embassy. She spoke of it with her usual clarity and poetic vigor, and late in the afternoon I continued the discussion with her son, Bertrand. What is even more striking, two or three days ago an Italian engineer and an Italian officer, who had just arrived from Japan, came to see me, and without much ado they proposed to me the problem in the following terms: "Father Allegra, we both come from good Catholic families, even though we may not be practicing Catholics. We have both received a good university training inspired by the principles of our faith, since we are graduates of Milan Sacred Heart University, whose ideal is to show in a concrete way that religion and science, far from being in conflict, are complementary to one another. But recently a friend of ours, a Buddhist, who knows and admires Père Teilhard and who specializes in the study of radium, has somewhat disturbed us. He told us that there are other inhabited worlds in the universe and that no religion, if we except Buddhism, can be made to agree with the findings of science. Buddhism, it is true, is not concerned with science, but it devotes its attention almost exclusively to the alleviation of human suffering. In such a vast universe and with so many inhabited worlds, what can be the place of Christ? Or, more specifically, is there still any place for Christ? And if so, what relation have all these possible rational beings to Christ?"

I first thought of sending them over to you, but since they had to leave for Shanghai on a Japanese military plane and could not postpone the trip, I tried to answer their questions by explaining to them two passages from St. Paul, namely, Colossians 1:16-17: "All things were created through him and for him..., and he holds all things in unity," and the other, Hebrews 1:2-3: "... the Son that he has appointed to inherit everything and through whom he made everything there is. He is... sustaining the universe by his powerful command." I must say that when they left me, they were happy and satisfied and, what is even more important, confirmed in their faith. They also told me something that seems to confirm the truth of your saying: that the Church needs a cosmic theology. I have even tried to explain to them, as clearly as I could, what you told me about the tree of life, the expansion of the universe, the Omega point, and the like. Perhaps you will laugh at it, but I had the impression that these little sparks of your scientific knowledge had an even greater effect on them than all my exegetical explanations.

Teilhard. I don't laugh out of pity — what would happen to the courtesy taught by St. Francis? — but because I rejoice at your attempt, the first of its kind, to integrate in all Franciscan modesty the data of cosmogenesis, orthogenesis, and anthropogenesis into the "Christification" of the universe. When I see Archbishop Zanin, I will tell him, with your permission, about this interesting and significant episode.

Allegra. I hope, Père Teilhard, that you will allow me to express my feelings with three lines of Dante:

> A great flame may follow a little spark;
> perhaps after me, with a better voice,
> prayers will be made to which Cyrrha
>   may respond.
>
> (*Paradiso*, I, 34-36)

Father, I believe you have opened a new way and that this will be followed. There will no doubt be hesitations, advances, and setbacks; powerful and brilliant minds will be needed; perhaps at the beginning few people will understand this new way which, in my opinion, is the necessary integration of "hyperphysics" with philosophy and theology; but this is the broad, new way upward that leads to *le Grand Christ.* Do not be surprised, Father, if its novelty, the terminology which is not always free from ambiguity, and the demands of an intellectual and moral order that it makes on those who want to follow it, may force the Church authorities to distrust it and put the simple faithful, all the faithful, on their guard. The new way will prevail in the end.

Teilhard. Are you perhaps referring to the attitude of Archbishop Zanin? I understand the reasons for it and I am fully aware of his fatherly love. In the meantime I want to thank you once more for what you have told me with complete frankness and honesty. I have known for many years that this would be my lot, and yet my passion and earnest desire to read the ways of God in the universe have kept me trying and have spurred me on. [*Digression of a personal nature.*] The vision of the universe which I have arrived at is not completely clear in all its details, but as a whole it fascinates me, and when I think that all things have as their beginning, center, and end *le Grand Christ,* I am literally dazzled.

The first "fulguration" that made me feel the scientific research as a revelation of the Creator was the realization that there are essential relationships between cosmogenesis, biogenesis, and noogenesis; that there is among them interdependence and co-finality; and that we can therefore speak of orthogenesis. This word stands for that finalistic evolution that stretches along a trajectory of millions and billions of years until, with the noosphere, a new era begins on earth. This is the era of the *homo sapiens*, who has the power to universalize, to foresee, and to provide. Man, by virtue of his reflex consciousness — man knows that he knows, he has what may be called consciousness to the second power — grows and develops in an ascending process toward totalization, which is the crowning of much effort and pain, the painful childbirth, as it were, of evolution.

After this war, no matter how distressing the condition of mankind may be, the process toward totalization will grow faster, for we are now in its compressive phase, the convergence of the "reflex." Totalization, in turn, will lead toward "unanimization," just as millions of years before now, the geological factors led to "hominization." As you see, in this ascent man is both the axle and the spoke, and in both capacities he tends toward the Omega point, Christ, *le Grand Christ*. I think that St. Paul is not only not against me but rather on my side. I hope you will be able to confirm my conviction by explaining his thought to me.

Allegra. Father, I will begin by saying that just as St. Paul speaks of God, Creator and Father, as being "all in all things" (I Cor. 15:28), so he uses the same expression in regard to Christ when he writes to the Colossians (3:11): "Christ is all things and in all." Likewise St. John says of God, the Creator and Father, that he is the Alpha and the Omega (Apoc. 1:8), and he then affirms the same thing of Christ. Here are the two principal texts. In the Apocalypse 1:17-18, Jesus thus speaks to the Apostle: "Do not be afraid; I am the First and the Last, and he who lives; I was dead, and behold, I am living forevermore"; and in Chapter 22:12-13, of the same mysterious book, Jesus speaks once more in the following terms: "Behold, I come quickly! And my reward is with me, to render to each one according to his works. I am the Alpha and the Omega, the First and the Last, the beginning and the end."

As far as St. Paul is concerned, I do not want to insist too much on the text of the letter to the Colossians 3:11, which seems to bear the following interpretation: "Just as the head is everything to the body, so that without it the body cannot live, so it is with the members of the mystical body of Christ: without distinction of race or social condition, they have in it their own dignity of sons by adoption. Without their head, Christ, from whom all graces come, without their being united with him, so that they live in him and he in them, they are not living but dead, they are condemned to death." However, if we consider the laws of the psychology of language and of the writer who uses it, it is not without reason, I will say with Père Bover, that St. Paul speaks of Christ in the same way he speaks of God the Father.

The position of St. John is even stronger. He gives the title of Alpha and Omega both to God the Father and Creator and to Christ. Christ is the Alpha, in the sense explained in another text of the Apocalypse (3:14): *"E arche tes ktiseos tou Theou"* (the beginning of the creation of God). Christ is the Omega inasmuch as he is the end for which all things have been made and to which all beings tend throughout the centuries.

Teilhard. Father, Sacred Scripture teaches the most profound truths in the most simple words. Whether it is idyl or cosmic drama, the world has meaning only in Christ. I have said idyl or cosmic drama, because one of the objections raised against my theory is that I deny the drama, the reality of human tragedy, and allow myself to be driven entirely by a sort of naïve optimism. But then what about St. Francis and his *Canticle of the Sun?* Is he not an optimist? Does not the revealed doctrine of Christ as Alpha and Omega encourage us to be optimists? Alpha and Omega means to measure, if that is possible, in terms of millions and billions of light-years, the instant in which the first creature appeared in relation to the whole of eternity.

St. John joins together that beginning and that end in the "Great Christ." What a sublime thought! My Omega point is not so much the terminus as it is the finality of orthogenesis. One can arrive at this — at least I believe I do — through the study of the phenomenon.

Allegra. Père Teilhard, that is true, but you study the phemonenon with the mind — and what a mind! — of a philosopher and a theologian. Even granting that you may not have the knowledge of many professors of theology, your approach is what makes the difference. But, getting back to St. Paul through St. John, I would like to point out that when the beloved Apostle writes to the churches of Asia that Christ is "the beginning of the creation of God," he merely confirms the teaching of St. Paul to the Ephesians and the Colossians, especially the latter, in the letter he sent to them from his Roman prison. If you allow me, I will read the passage from the letter to the Colossians (1:15-20) and, following the interpretation of many exegetes, I will tell you in brief what I believe to be its most evident meaning. I cannot conceal the fact, however, that a strong exegetical trend headed by St. Thomas Aquinas, the prince of theologians, and Estius,[52] a renowned commentator on St. Paul's epistles, gives a different explanation from the one I would like to submit with modesty but also with Pauline *parresia.*

In the powerful and illuminating text that I have just mentioned (Col. 1:15-20), St. Paul speaks of Christ in relation to God, creatures, and the Church. As far as his relation to God is concerned, Christ is said to be the living image of the invisible Father, who lives in inaccessible light, so that he who sees Christ, not so much with bodily eyes as with the eyes of faith, sees also the Father. As for his relation to creatures, Christ is called by St. Paul "the firstborn." The patristic explanation of this title is almost unanimously accepted, especially when compared to Christ's other title, "the only-begotten." Christ is called "the only-begotten" inasmuch as he is the Son of God; he is called "the firstborn" insofar as he is the Son of man: *"Mediator Dei et hominum, homo Christus Jesus"* (There is one mediator between God and men, himself a man, Christ Jesus — I Tim. 2:5). He is the firstborn not so much because of the unique excellence deriving to him from his hypostatic union, but rather because he is the beginning of God's operations *ad extra*, i. e., outside himself. He is the first-willed among all created beings. Furthermore, all beings have been willed and created for him and because of him, and in him alone they have their consistency: *"Kai ta panta en auto sunesteken."* Christ's relation to the Church is evident from the fact that he is its head. He is the principle that communicates divine life to the Church, for in him there is the fullness of divinity and grace. It is through his blood that he acquired the beloved Spouse whom he continues to purify and sanctify.

To hold with many exegetes — in fact, the majority of them — that St. Paul speaks first of the preexistent Word of God and then of the Incarnate Word, is in my opinion to do violence to the Greek construction and particularly to the Apostle's thought. Indeed, St. Paul speaks of the Son of God both as Incarnate and as Redeemer, who has been absolutely willed by God the Father before the foundation of the world; so he teaches in his letter to the Ephesians. He speaks of the "Beloved" (*egapemenos*) in whom, before the world was made, God blessed us, chose us, and predestined us to be his adoptive sons. He has enriched us with his grace and with the fullness of Christ. In Christ, by virtue of his blood, we have been redeemed, have received the remission of our sins and the revelation of the mystery of his will, and have been stamped with the seal of the Holy Spirit of the promise. And all of this has been done for the praise of the glory of God (Eph. 1:1-14).

Christ's coming into the world was not determined by Adam's sin, nor was the world created casually or incidentally. On the contrary, the world exists for Christ and because of Christ. It is Christ, I would say, who is the occasion, or rather the cause of the existence of the world, which in him alone has consistency. It is he who reveals and glorifies the Father and is the head of creation, which, through his Incarnation, has been consecrated and continues to be consecrated by his Church, the continuation of Christ that transcends time and space. To draw the ultimate consequences of St. Paul's thought, one might even say that creation is perennially consecrated by the Eucharist, both as a sacrifice, inasmuch as it mystically perpetuates the oblation of the Calvary, and as a sacrament which mystically perpetuates Christ's presence until his second coming. As a sacrament, the Eucharist is also the sure sign of Christ's presence in the world and the indisputable pledge that he is truly Emmanuel, i. e., God with us.

Père Teilhard, this seems to me the mind of St. Paul — the man struck by lightning who, on the way to Damascus, beheld the glory of the resurrected, heavenly Christ, the Christ who ascended to the right hand of the Father to fulfill all things (*ut impleret omnia*). I do not hesitate to say that St. Paul really gives us the cosmic dimensions of Christ, *le Grand Christ*, and not merely those Mediterranean dimensions that many Christians attribute to him.[53]

Teilhard. Maranatha! Come, our Lord! Yes, by all means, this is the teaching of St. Paul. In the light of this cosmic Christ, the universal Christ, all the objections raised by contemporary science vanish into nothing.

Allegra. That is the exact word: they vanish. It is on the basis of this kind of exegesis that I did not find it difficult to answer the questions of my two Italian friends who, because of the ever-increasing dimensions of the universe and the possibility of the existence of other inhabited worlds, had entertained some doubts about their faith. In fact, the universe and all rational beings existing in it are linked to Christ, since they are all created for him and they all depend on him.

The Incarnation is the supreme work of God, and therefore it cannot be repeated. It is toward the Incarnation that all things, including time and space, converge. The Incarnate Word holds primacy over all beings, and to him they owe existence, grace, and glory, each one according to its own nature. This is so, regardless of whether these beings are on our planet, in our solar system, or in some other planetary system on the edges of the universe, and regardless of whether they are angels, men, or rational beings different from us. Recapitulation — this is a poor translation of the Greek word *anakephalaiosis* — must not be understood, so it seems to me, merely in a soteriological sense, but rather in a cosmic sense (Eph. 1:10). I find this same doctrine in the prologue of St. Paul's letter to the Hebrews: "God ... spoke to our ancestors through his Son, the Son that he has appointed to inherit everything and through whom he made everything there is. He is the radiant light of God's glory and the perfect copy of his nature, sustaining the universe by his powerful command; and now that he has destroyed the defilement of sin, he has gone to take his place in heaven at the right hand of divine Majesty" (Heb. 1:2-3).

My dear Père Teilhard, I know that today this entire Pauline thought is explained in terms of the preexisting Word and not of the Incarnate Word. I am also aware that the Iranists[54] find the origin of this thought in the *Urmensch,* and many followers of the comparative method of the history of religions see in the later St. Paul (Ephesians, Colossians, Hebrews) Stoic and Gnostic doctrines that the Apostle would have unsuccessfully tried to apply to Christ. Consequently, either the Pauline authenticity of these letters is denied, or they are explained in terms of an erudition that frightens Catholic interpreters who entrench themselves behind the doctrine of the preexisting Word. Yet, if St. Paul could only make his interpreters understand that his Christ, the Incarnate Son of God, is the Alpha and Omega of the universe, they would be able to overcome without too much difficulty the aforesaid theories.

I have the impression, however, that both exegesis and biblical theology are now being directed toward the doctrine of the absolute primacy of Christ, a direction that hopefully they will be forced to take either because of a more accurate study of the book of Wisdom in the

Old Testament, or because of the harmony of the two Testaments, or finally, because of findings concerning Gnosticism and Stoicism in the Christian era. It is not altogether impossible that a better study of certain rabbinical texts to the effect that God has created the world for and because of the Messiah, may also show that Paul, the disciple of Rabban Gamaliel, after he was struck on the road to Damascus and after his ascent to the third heaven, was endowed with such supernatural power of vision as to be able to contemplate the undisclosed mystery of Christ and reveal it to us. I may add that if theologians follow the fantastic progress of the sciences, even from afar and somewhat as amateurs, they will sooner or later have to heed the doctrine of Christ as Alpha and Omega, as king of the universe, who, like God the Father, is in St. Paul's words all in all things—*"ina genetai en pasin autos proteuon"* (that in all things he may have the first place—Col. 1:18).

Teilhard. Thank you, Father, for all you have told me. With such a theology one not only can feel more at ease, but he can also advance and progress. You Franciscans should continue to defend and propagate even more earnestly than you have done until now the doctrine of the primacy of Christ, just as you have done for centuries in regard to the dogma of the Immaculate Conception. Indeed, I am convinced, and

I insist on it, that from now on the Church has "to feel" a cosmic Christ and that she "needs" a cosmic theology.

Allegra. Father, I would rather expect your Society to come forth and defend this noblest and worthiest of causes. By reason of its high level of culture, its large number of scientists, and wonderful organization, I think one ought to expect even more from your Society than from us.

Teilhard. That is how it should be. But don't forget what I told you about the way Galileo's heliocentric theory was received by his contemporaries and immediate successors, even though that doctrine was to supersede the centuries-old geocentric theory.

Allegra. Père Teilhard, I believe that in the field of theology Christocentrism or Christofinalism, as taught by St. Paul and St. John, ought not to supersede but to integrate the soteriological doctrinal system in a broader vision that is more worthy of the mission of Christ. In such an integration the traditional soteriology would not only remain intact, but would undoubtedly present to us in a much brighter light and much more convincingly Christ's love for his heavenly Father and for men, his brethren. To this effect it is necessary to coordinate in a harmonious synthesis all the data of revelation, such as the Trinitarian doctrine, the intimate life of God, the absolute primacy of Christ, and the mystery of the Cross, with the light, also of divine origin, that comes from science. Perhaps what at one time was attempted by the great medieval schoolmen and, as far as the absolute primacy of Christ is concerned, by Scotus, St. Bernardine of Siena, St. Lawrence of Brindisi, and St. Francis de Sales, has become today a frightening and seemingly impossible undertaking because of the large amount of scientific research that it involves. Yet the construction of a complete theological system that presents in its proper light not merely one aspect but all the aspects of revelation, the whole truth that, in the words of Dante, so much ennobles and elevates us (*"la verità che tanto ci sublima"*),[55] is the definite task of theology in the imminent future.

Teilhard. This has also been my conviction for years. Do you know Père Charles[56] and Père Huby?[57]

Allegra. I do not know them personally, but I have read Charles' work, *La prière de toutes les heures*, and Huby's *Christus*, his manual of the history of religions, as well as his commentary on the Gospel of St. Mark, which, if I correctly recall, I found in the collection *Verbum salutis.*

Teilhard. Well, some years ago I asked both of them, but especially Père Charles, to study this fascinating theme (*argument ravissant*) of the primacy or Pleroma of Christ; but either because of their many other commitments, or because —

so I was told — the time was not yet ripe, very little has been done in this area.

[At this point Père Teilhard, in answer to one of my questions which I do not recall exactly at this moment, made a digression and presented me with a copy of his essay *Fossil Men: Recent Discoveries and Present Problems,* published in Peking by Henry Vetch in 1943, and spoke to me in clear and proper terms of the evolution of the human species. He gave a detailed account of the discovery of the Sinanthropus which took place at Choukoutien, and made a thorough evaluation of this 100,000-year-old ancestor of man whom he defined as *homo faber* and *homo sapiens*. I listened to his passionate account as attentively as one who is not particularly competent in that field could do, until Père Teilhard, if I recall aright, began to talk about the transformation of the anthropoids. At that point, without my being aware of it, I must have shown a greater interest in the subject and become more recollected, for he interrupted his talk and said to me: *"Vous avez une mine assez méditative"* (You seem to be rather concerned today). Then he continued:] What is the reason? Don't you think that the transformation and evolution I am talking about can lead to Christ?

Allegra. Oh, yes, I think it may, and yet I am not quite sure of it.

Teilhard. Please, speak out your mind with Pauline *parresia*.

Allegra. I will, Father. What strikes me in your description of the endless ascending process of the human species, as though this must have begun almost simultaneously and silently (*sans bruit*) on many distant points of our planet, is that I do not find in it three most important facts of our Christian revelation. I refer to those three points of criticism which I made in my written report as censor for Archbishop Zanin and which I showed to you at the time of our first meeting. Today I have felt even more strongly the contrast between dogmatic theology, as I have studied it, and the data of science, as expounded by you. Permit me to develop my thought further, for it is my conviction that we are not dealing merely with a *quodlibetum* or *quaestio disputata* (a disputed question),[58] but with the fundamental doctrine of God's redemptive plan and Christian anthropology.

Teilhard. Please go ahead.

Allegra. Well, in your theory I do not see how it is possible to save the doctrine of the unity of mankind and its elevation to the supernatural order from which it fell as a result of original sin. Consequently, I do not find a place—I mean a central place—for Redemption, for the Cross of Christ. The ways of God, as we know them by revelation, and the ways of man, known to us through the sciences, must meet. However, I am afraid that if we accept your ascending and descending biological theory, we cannot avoid a clash between the ways of God and the ways of man.

To obtain more information on the subject, I went to the library of Petang—the Catholic rectory in the northern section of Peking—to consult the article on "Polygenism" in the *Dictionnaire de théologie catholique*.[59] It seems to me that the two authors who have signed it are aware of the theological difficulty of reconciling that theory with the doctrine of original sin. The suppression of this doctrine seems to shake, or at least greatly weaken, one of the foundations of St. Paul's soteriology: *primus Adam, novus Adam* (the first Adam, the new Adam). Likewise, without the wound inflicted on human nature by original sin, it becomes difficult to explain the struggle between the *mysterium iniquitatis* (the mystery of iniquity) and the kingdom of God that began in Eden. And what about the history, always present, of this struggle—witness the Apocalypse—of which we are the sad spectators and which might become worse before the second coming of our Lord? I must confess, however, that because of being cut off by the war, as we are here in Peking, from all biblical, philosophical, and theological research, all I have said must be understood in the light of my past studies, some of which are perhaps outdated by this time. I hope, Father, that you will forgive my frankness.[60]

Teilhard. There is no need for forgiveness; instead, I am very grateful to you for your frankness and I will try to repay you in kind. First of all, I would like to point out that the mere omission of the doctrine of original sin, which does not belong to the study of the phenomenon of man, is not the same thing as its denial. By vocation I am a scientist; I study human fossils and draw from this study the conclusions that are imposed upon me. In so doing, I am convinced that I serve both the cause of truth and the cause of God. My only wish is that theologians may not be short-sighted, but, rather, willing to reconsider revealed data in the light of truths of other orders, too, such as are in our case the truths of the scientific order. *Light cannot extinguish light.* Think for a moment, Father, of the biblical chronology. I believe that today no exegete worthy of the name would assign six thousand years of life to the human species, defend the universality of the flood, or accept the account of the origin of the different languages as narrated in the book of Genesis in connection with the construction of the tower of Babel. Some Scripture scholar has told me that the account of the ten plagues of Egypt and of the passage across the Red Sea can perhaps be given a less miraculous explanation. From this you can guess what is my thought. These and other similar problems were not and could not have been raised by the Fathers and Doctors of the Church in their lifetime. Nor could they have been raised up to the last century or, let us say, Galileo's century. But when science forced those problems upon the theologians, they had to face them and, after a period of hesitation and controversy, they had to solve them in accordance with the unquestionable data of science.

You might object that those were after all only marginal problems. I agree with you as far as the age of the human species is concerned, or such other issues as the historical value of the account of the tower of Babel, a universal flood, the plagues of Egypt, and the subsequent passage across the Red Sea. But when cosmogony and anthropogenesis are at stake, then you must admit that these are not merely marginal problems. As for the biblical account of these doctrines, I am inclined to believe that the Bible is a sublime religious narrative of a popular character that must be implemented with the data of science. Science, in turn, must follow its own way and methods of research without any view to supporting a particular system of thought or any prejudicial attitude. With this kind of spirit and independent attitude, the scientist will arrive in his work at certain definite conclusions which the theologian has to take into account and integrate into his own system. Think, for example, of the true scientific revolution that took place after Galileo, and also — but here I speak merely as an observer — of the more universal and human concept of international law that has developed as a result of the discovery of America.

You are no doubt aware of the fact that many theologians, perhaps the great majority of them, show a striking erudition in regard to peripheric questions, whereas they are completely shortsighted in regard to the most important problems of cosmogenesis, anthropogenesis, Christ the Pleroma, i. e., the universal Christ, or, as you prefer to say, the absolute primacy of Christ. In my essay *La parole attendue*, I have endeavored to express what are my expectations of theology in the future. [Here Père Teilhard read to me some passages from his essay and put special emphasis on the following statements: "The Pleroma: this is the mysterious synthesis of the uncreated and the created, the full completion, both quantitative and qualitative, of the universe in God. It is impossible to read St. Paul without being at once struck by the fundamental importance he attaches to this notion taken in its most absolute realism, the comparatively obscure place in which it has been left until now by preachers and theologians, and its wonderful appropriateness to the religious needs of the present time."]

Who knows? Perhaps an Ecumenical Council will give the Church the refreshing new vitality that is suitable to the exciting epoch in which we live and in which we shall have to live more and more.

Allegra. Père Teilhard, your reflections have led me to think of Pascal, Dante, and Voltaire.

Teilhard. Of Voltaire? *Mais vous êtes épatant!* (But this really surprises me!)[61]

Allegra. Yes, Father, of Voltaire, and I hope you will not be scandalized. Since I have permission to read forbidden books, I borrowed from Professor Vargas an extremely interesting Voltaire anthology in which I came across a thought that struck me: "The most tedious books are those which pretend to explain everything." This statement is true but incomplete; it should contain its counterpart: "The most useful books are those which stimulate the reader to think for himself." Now Dante and Pascal make me think, and I can assure you that your words today will also make me think, and think a lot! Thank you for your present.

Teilhard. I should thank you rather for having understood me so well. Yes, it cannot be otherwise: *Light cannot extinguish light.* However, I would like to add one more thing. Your objection to the Parousia which I discuss toward the end of my book has seemed to me to be somewhat affected by staticism. And yet you seem to have such a sensibility and intuition of the revealed truth that you ought to be able to understand those clear, although brief, statements of St. Paul in his letter to the Romans, Chapter 8, verse 22: *"Omnis creatura ingemiscit et parturit usque adhuc"* (All creation groans and travails in pain until now), and elsewhere: *"Nolumus expoliari sed supervestiri"* (We do not wish to be unclothed, but rather clothed over — II Cor. 5:4). I am sure you have grasped my thought. What do you think of it?

Allegra. Yes, it is true that I have been reticent on this point, but that is due to the nature of the subject, the eschatology, of which the Parousia is but a moment, albeit the greatest and most glorious moment. This is not an easy subject. As you know, Père Teilhard, the eschatological doctrine involves many serious difficulties. We have in the Synoptics the eschatological discourse, whose true meaning has not yet been fully revealed to us, whereas in the fourth Gospel the subject is reduced to its strictly essential points. If we turn to the Apocalypse and the two letters of St. Paul to the Thessalonians — I leave aside the few hints the Apostle gives here and there in other letters — we notice that the supreme moment or climax of eschatology, i. e., the Parousia of our Lord, is described with such an abundance of symbols and allegories that all one can say for certain is what is contained in the Apostles' Creed. As for the remaining questions, the exegetes are not of one mind in their interpretations.

This will give you an idea why, after having made my reservations on the meaning of Redemption, I thought it better simply to mention the fact that the Parousia is presented as a natural complement of anthropogenesis. Assuming that man "always advances and proceeds further," that he ascends and converges toward the ultra-human, the Omega point, and that such a converging ascent is due to the action of the Evolver (*Evoluteur*) of the cosmos through the process of cosmogenesis and anthropogenesis, "the Great Christ," it follows logically that you should present the Parousia as the critical evolving point of collective maturation, or, should I say, as the natural terminus of the finalistic evolution of the human species. There must be some truth in this optimistic description of the Parousia, but I do not think that it includes all revealed truth.

Teilhard. Look, Father Allegra, the contemplation of the world has been until recently static, theocentric as well as anthropocentric; but today man has adopted an aggressive and exclusively anthropocentric attitude toward the world, and even the few believing scientists have ceased to see in creation the great sign of God. We must replace staticism — we are already doing it every day — with the dynamism of the cosmogenesis and anthropogenesis, a dynamism in which man, especially the Christian, is called to participate. Does not this remind you of the preface of my book? Now, if at this point we bring on the scene the Pauline thought that the Redemption is a new creation, *kaine ktisis,* if we mitigate our Western individualism, if we reflect that this new creation is the work of the Incarnate Word, the great Evolver, *le Grand Christ,* and, finally, if we try to understand that the evolution of humanity throughout thousands and thousands of years corresponds to the plan of God the Creator, I dare to say, Father, that my notion of the Parousia does not seem to contradict the data of revelation.

Allegra. Père Teilhard, I do not speak, nor did I speak, of contradiction, but rather of absence and incompleteness, and my doubts continue to persist. It seems to me that your vision of the world as a whole contains a good deal of truth and novelty that helps us to read and understand the Bible better; but before it is integrated into that cosmic theology toward which we are both looking, it must be perfected. The whole *Itinerarium mentis in Deum* of St. Bonaventure can perhaps be summed up in one sentence of his Commentary on Ecclesiastes: "Every creature is a word of God because it speaks of God."[62] It is quite possible that you wish to say the same thing in modern scientific terms. If this is the case, I fully endorse your statement that a Christian ought to be attentive to the voice of God, regardless of whether it comes from creatures or from revelation. Creation and revelation are after all both from God and, as you said, light does not extinguish light; on the contrary, when a light is brought closer to another light it becomes even brighter. Today I cannot go further; but I promise you that, as far as possible, I will lend my attentive ears to the voice of God in his creatures.

PART THREE

Teilhard. Do you know, Father Allegra, that you have motivated me to page once more through the works of Pascal, Dante, and Voltaire? I did this at our library of Tientsin, which is rather large and which I know very well from years of study. I am not too familiar with our library at Maison Chabanel. What a man, that Voltaire! *Quelle verve endiablée!* (What devilish ardor!) And what lucid language . . . , the cold lucidity of the blasphemer! It is only to be regretted that in that century the Church in France had no one who could match his writing. What the Church needed was a man like Pascal! . . . Unfortunately, I do not know Italian well enough to appreciate the poetry of the Supreme Poet, but with the aid of Lamennais' translation I can manage it.

As for Pascal, that is, as far as Pascal's thought is concerned, I am not at all pleased with the Jansenistic pessimism that pervades it; nor do I share his dread of the silence of the infinite heavenly spaces. On the contrary, this apparent silence—for in the heavenly spaces, in the starry oceans, in the innumerable galaxies there is a fantastic, unimaginable, vertiginous life—excites me and throws me on my knees, because I see how true, even from the physical viewpoint, is the word of God: *"Pater meus usque modo operatur, et ego operor"* (My Father goes on working, and so do I—John 5:17). It is a question here of the creative act that continues and is being intensified, that rises and converges toward the Omega point, toward the Great Christ, the cosmic Christ. The universe is but his Pleroma, his royal mantle. Dante is more optimistic than Pascal and knows better how to stay at the center of the Christian mystery. Tell me, Father, which *Cantica* of the *Divine Comedy* do you prefer, and why?

Allegra. Père Teilhard, in all three of them there is the lion's imprint and sometimes I feel at a loss in deciding which is the best: whether the *Inferno*, the *Purgatorio*, or the *Paradiso*. However, I tend toward having a strong preference for the *Paradiso*, of which Cardinal Manning wrote: *"Post Dantis paradisum nihil restat nisi visio Dei"* (After one has read Dante's *Paradiso*, there remains nothing but the vision of God).[63] In it the feeble human word becomes light, fire, and melody. Some of the verses of the *Paradiso* appear to me as the loftiest and most profound words ever written by a human being; they are as concise and direct as an oracle, and *"solo amore e luce han per confine"* (they have only light and love for boundaries—*Paradiso*, XXVIII, 54). I may add here that some of those words were the delight of St. Bernardine of Siena, St. Francis de Sales, Pius IX, and a host of others.

Teilhard. I can imagine how delighted my good friend Père Valensin would be if only he had the opportunity to meet you! I am sure you would likewise enjoy the meeting, for Père Valensin has a profound knowledge of the *Divine Comedy,* which he considers to be like a *Summa* of theology, philosophy, and poetry. How convincingly does he say now and then: *"Oh, mon Dante!"* (Ah, my Dante!) But please tell me which are the verses you like the most.

Allegra. Father, more than my liking them, they are to me — to use a Dantean expression — my "vital nourishment." I will confine myself to quoting a few verses that glorify God as Love.

> ... O Love who rulest heaven.
>
> *(Paradiso,* I, 74)

> And we will direct our eyes to
> the First Love.
>
> *(Paradiso,* XXXII, 142)

> Not to acquire any benefit, which
>   cannot be,
> but in order that Its splendor
> might declare as It shines, '*Sub-
>   sisto*' [I am],
> the Eternal Love, in Its eternity,
>   outside of Time

> and every other limitation, as It
> pleased,
> disclosed Itself in new loves
> [angels].
>
> *(Paradiso,* XXIX, 13-18)

And there are many, many other verses which marvelously uplift the soul of the Christian:

> ... We have advanced
> from the greatest body to the
> Heaven of pure light,
> a light intellectual, full of love,
> love of the good, replete with
> joy,
> a joy that transcends all sweetness.
>
> *(Paradiso,* XXX, 38-42)

[Here we engaged for a while in a conversation that was at once both Dantean and biblical in character, as we were both trying to find in the Scriptures the foundation for Dante's thought. From the Scriptures we turned to St. Francis of Assisi, especially his *Canticle of the Sun,* then to St. Augustine, and finally to Scotus, as we began to read Father Gerard Manley Hopkins' poem "Duns Scotus' Oxford." I must confess that, as I was talking, I was delighted to see Père Teilhard in such high spirits and so overwhelmed with joy. At the end of our conversation he said to me:]

Teilhard. Father Allegra, don't think for a moment that we have wandered from our subject. I am sure you understand me, for you have noticed with great satisfaction that in my work *The Divine Milieu* I speak of God and his Christ as *l'Aimant et l'Aimable* (the Lover and the Lovable). Thus I simply follow along the line of St. Paul, St. John, St. Francis of Assisi, Duns Scotus, and Dante.

Allegra. I have not only noticed that, but I have also noticed the fact that in your work, perhaps without realizing it, you follow the same procedure as Scotus does in his *De primo principio*.[61] After a series of profound and difficult metaphysical arguments, overcome, as it were, by the love of God, Scotus addresses himself to the Supreme Being with such ardent prayers that Father Longpré did not hesitate to call Scotus' work the fruit of his mystical union. I have read again and again the prayers of *The Divine Milieu*, and I can assure you that I really enjoyed them. I do not wish to go any further for fear that you might get even the slightest impression that I am flattering you.

To get back now to your expression *l'Aimant et l'Aimable*, I would like to point out that in the works of Duns Scotus with which I am familiar, there is a fundamental thought that in my opinion explains his entire theological synthesis: it enlightens it from within and makes it extremely appealing and fascinating. Perhaps instead of one fundamental thought I should speak of several fundamental thoughts. More specifically, we are confronted with a truth that is grasped almost intuitively or by contemplation, and that is presented to us by the Subtle Doctor in its various aspects as in the different colors of a prism. The reader who is not able to discover that fundamental thought, or rather those fundamental thoughts, becomes bored by the depth and subtlety of Scotus' reasoning; and unless he himself is a metaphysical genius, he will prefer the crystal clarity of St. Thomas' *Summa theologica* or the soft, sweet, and harmonious prose of St. Bonaventure. Briefly, Scotus, like St. Paul, is not an easy author. However, the reader who is able to discover those fundamental thoughts I refer to, is like one who has found the key to a chest filled with the most valuable treasures. Far from being bored, he will appreciate the depth and sublimity of Scotus' genius and engage with him, as it were, in a most fruitful dialogue.

Teilhard. Tell me, then, about those fundamental thoughts, for on account of my many occupations I may not be able to hear or read about them again. As you know, by repeating over and over again two of his key ideas, Bergson has succeeded in convincing a large number of people. Although I do not quite agree with what he says, I must admit that when he speaks or writes he is fascinating. [Here a digression was made to discuss the thought of Bergson and Blondel. At the end of the discussion, Father apologized to me and said: *"Je suis en faute; maintenant c'est à vous de parler"* (I am at fault; now it is your turn to speak).]

Allegra. Père Teilhard, I have here with me the *Summula Scotistica* of Diomede Scaramuzzi, as well as *Ioannis Duns Scoti doctrina philosophica et theologica* by Parthenius Minges. If you don't mind, before synthesizing the Christocentric doctrine of Scotus, I would like to read to you the passages containing the fundamental principles I have previously mentioned.

God is love by his very essence: "God is formally love and formally charity, and not merely the cause of love."[65] This is Scotus' first principle, and it can be brought close to his other principle concerning God's infinity: "The concept of an infinite being includes many things virtually. Just as being includes virtually in itself goodness and truth, so an infinite being includes infinite truth and infinite goodness, as well as every other pure perfection to an infinite degree."[66] Now let us retain the principle that God's infinity implies the total and comprehensive presence of all the divine attributes or perfections. If, then, we ask why God is boundless, immutable, incomprehensible, omniscient, and omnipotent, our invariable answer must be this: 'Because he is infinite.' If we accept this doctrine of Scotus, it follows that God is essentially infinite Love, and consequently, as Manzoni says, 'all-powerful Love.' You may see the results of this principle throughout theology: in it are contained the absolute primacy of Christ and the redemption by means of pure, ardent, infinite love. I would like now to read a page from Scotus in which his powerful mind penetrates the mysterious depths of this doctrine and brings out many points that are extremely enlightening. Am I boring you, Father?

Teilhard. Not at all. Please continue.

[Père Teilhard followed with his eyes the text of the *Summula Scotistica* as I read to him from the beginning of the third section of paragraph 1, p. 174: *"Item, si lapsus esset causa praedestinationis Christi,"* up to the concluding words of paragraph 3, p. 176: *"nisi redemptio fuisset facienda":*]

"Had the fall [of Adam] been the cause of the predestination of Christ, then the supreme work of God would have been merely incidental. Now, it seems most unreasonable to maintain that God would have forgone such a masterpiece simply because of a [hypothetical] good deed of Adam, such as it would have been if Adam had not sinned. The glory of all creatures can indeed never be as intensively great as the glory of Christ.

"Therefore, I argue this way: First, God loves himself; in the second place, he loves himself in others, and this is pure love; in the third place, he wants to be loved by another who can love him to the highest degree, inasmuch as that is possible to a being outside himself; and finally, he foresees the [hypostatic] union of that nature which ought to love him to the highest degree even if man had not fallen.

"This is then the order in the foreknowledge of God: First, God knows himself as the supreme good; secondly, he knows all other beings and creatures; thirdly, he predestines to glory and grace [those who are to be saved], while in a purely negative way he does not predestine the others; fourthly, he has foreknowledge of all those who would fall as a result of the sin of Adam; and finally, he foresees and preordains the remedy [for sin], namely, that men would be redeemed through the passion of his Son. Thus the Christ-man, as well as all the elect, was foreseen and predestined to grace and glory even prior to foreseeing his passion as a remedy against the fall, just as a physician has a greater interest in the health of a patient than in prescribing medicine for him.

"Authorities [to the contrary] can all be explained in this sense: namely, that Christ would not have come as a Redeemer if man had not sinned. Perhaps, too, he would not have come in a body capable of suffering, since there would have been no need for his soul to be united to a passible body if no Redemption was necessary. The soul of Christ was, in effect, glorified from its very beginning and predestined by God not only to the highest glory but also to a glory that is coextensive with its existence."

[As I was reading from the *Summula*, every now and then Père Teilhard would help me with the French translation. When I finished my reading, he said emphatically:] It is a marvelous page! What a plain but unique power of expression. *Voilà la théologie cosmique, la théologie de l'avenir!* (There you have the cosmic theology, the theology of the future!) Let me ask you now to leave aside the text and summarize for me Scotus' thought, just as we have done with St. Paul.

Allegra. I shall try [and I did so with the help of a few notes which I had prepared beforehand].

The key statements of the Scotistic doctrine of the absolute primacy of Christ and of Redemption as a work of pure and ardent love, can be reduced to the following:

(a) "God's supreme work cannot be merely incidental."[67]

(b) "God willed to be loved by another who could love him to the highest degree, inasmuch as that is possible to a being outside of himself."⁶⁸

(c) "All the authoritative texts [of both Sacred Scripture and the Fathers of the Church] can be explained in this sense: namely, that Christ would not have come into this world *as a Redeemer* if the first man had not sinned."⁶⁹

(d) "I hold, therefore, that whatever has been done by Christ for our Redemption became necessary only because it had been so decreed by the divine will, and thus it became necessary for Christ to suffer only by reason of that decree.... We are therefore greatly indebted to him. Indeed, since man could have been redeemed otherwise, but nevertheless he [Christ] chose to redeem him in that way by an act of his free will, we are greatly indebted to him, and even more so than if it had been necessary for us to be redeemed that way and not otherwise. I believe he did that chiefly to impel us to love him and because he wanted man to be more closely bound to God."⁷⁰

(e) "Hence the Trinity does not bestow upon man in his present state any benefit pertaining to salvation except by reason of the offering of Christ on the cross, an offering that was made by the most lovable person and out of a supreme act of charity."⁷¹

In connection with the first statement, which for me has a crystal-clear lucidity [and also for me, added Père Teilhard at once], I would like to read to you the opinion of the Anglican convert Father Faber: "If Christ was decreed after us, and because of us, and only to redeem us, these three monstrous consequences follow: first, that Christ would owe us a debt of gratitude; secondly, that we should in certain respects be more excellent than he; and thirdly, that sin was necessary to his existence."[72] I may add that if sin and the ensuing Redemption were the occasion or, as some claim, the motive for the Incarnation, then all God's operations *ad extra* (outside himself) would converge on man, so that the end of God's activity *ad extra* would no longer be the manifestation and the communication of his own goodness but the salvation of mankind, as though God would not be able to achieve his external glorification except through the worship and love of the human creature. But what is after all the love of all angels and saints compared to the love of Christ for his Father, to the glory that the heart of Christ offers to his Father, to Christ's adoration of his Father?

Duns Scotus says that the sum-total of the glory of all creatures is not as intensively great as the glory of Christ, so that it is very unlikely that God would have forgone such a masterpiece if man had not sinned. I am sure that if St. Paul could come down from heaven and be questioned as to the motive of the Incarnation, he who preached that Christ holds the primacy in everything would most surely deny that the Word became flesh solely to redeem humanity, so that without sin there would be no Christ. How could that be if, according to his teaching, Christ is all in all things like God the Father, having the same "plenitude" of God?

Teilhard. Father, you are trying to translate into modern terms the theological metaphysics of the gigantic thinker who was John Duns Scotus, and I cannot but congratulate you on this. But if you had to speak *his qui foris sunt,* that is, to those who are outside the Church, I think you should go even further than that, for our theological vocabulary is beyond their comprehension. I see now that Scotus is truly a powerful thinker and that his texts manifest a genuine Pauline *parresia.* I have been told by Father Chanté that you have been invited to give a talk on Duns Scotus at our Maison Chantel. Isn't that correct?

Allegra. Yes, Father, that is right.

Teilhard. I beg you, then, to speak in strong and clear terms.

Allegra. Thank you, Father, for your advice, and thank you also for your suggestion to make Christian thought intelligible to the people of today. I must admit, however, that this is not an easy task; one should first know the people's mentality. Today I am not in a position to do that. I will therefore continue to speak in Scholastic terminology but in a rather popular way, following the notes that I have previously prepared. There is a contemporary Italian philosopher, Carmelo Ottaviano, who perhaps speaks the kind of language that you would like to see on the lips and in the writings of present-day Catholic priests. May I be allowed to read a page quoted by Scaramuzzi in which Professor Ottaviano illustrates the Scotistic principle: *"Summum bonum non potest esse occasionatum"* (The supreme good cannot be merely incidental)?

Teilhard. Please do so, and be sure to translate into French the statements of a more metaphysical nature.

Allegra. Professor Ottaviano writes: "If we look for the final purpose of nature and search deeply into nature itself, we cannot fail to discover the supernatural, in which nature is fully itself as in its efficient cause, and only such by its being itself. [Père Teilhard commented: *C'est génial; continuez* — This is the thought of a genius; please continue.] But Christ, the God-man, is the center and source of the supernatural. Christ is therefore at the center of all things. Christ is everywhere, while nature is such only upon the condition of being in Christ, transfigured and divinized in Christ. [*Teilhard. Très vrai* — It is very true.] Nature tends toward Christ in its becoming, and since the whole being of nature is in the process of becoming, it really is its becoming; thus nature is for Christ. The theology of the Franciscan school maintains that creation has been ordained to Christ the God-man, to the Incarnation, and hence to the supernatural as to its final cause. This is perfectly true. That is why the dazzled eyes of the great convert at Damascus, perhaps the most perfect Christian, saw Christ everywhere.... The whole of reality is like the fire, it flees upwards; that is its own life as it is the life of the fire, whose whole essence is to burn. Reality can be attained through Christ."[73]

Teilhard. That is all very true and is expressed in lucid and energetic terms. It seems to me that Professor Ottaviano tries to join in a bold synthesis certain ideas of Hegel and St. Augustine with the thought of Scotus and St. Paul.

Allegra. Father, I am not sure about Hegel, since I am not sufficiently acquainted with his thought, but I would say that St. Augustine has something to do with it, and even the Scholastics, although when they speak of the *potentia oboedientialis* of the creature, that is, the creature's capacity for a superior perfection, they refer to St. Augustine's teaching.

Teilhard. Look, Father, as far as I can see, Professor Ottaviano expresses in modern terms the same position I am defending. He speaks of the mutual complementary nature of the two orders, the natural and the supernatural, although, to judge from the page you have just read to me, he does not seem to realize that even creation in its real and concrete meaning, that which I call "sacred matter," demands Christ the Pleroma, Christ the Alpha and Omega. The integration of science, philosophy, and theology is bound to come. As for me, I am satisfied to be a modest pioneer, the humble messenger who will wait in his grave for the realization of the hopes I have expressed in my essay *La parole attendue*. But, Father, please continue.

Allegra. Père Teilhard, before expounding Scotus' second theme, *"Deus voluit ab alio summe diligi"* (God willed to be loved by another to the highest degree), I would first like to say with Pascal that there is no question here of the God of philosophers, but of the God who is also the Father of Jesus Christ, our Lord. Moreover, I would like to add, with Dante:

> This decree, my brother, lies buried
> to the eyes of everyone whose mind
> has not matured in the flames of love.
> (*Paradiso*, VII, 58-60)

Briefly, as St. Augustine says, he who loves will understand: *"Da amantem et sentit quod dico."*[74] It is not mere chance that the mystics and saints are especially motivated by this principle to accept and live the doctrine of the primacy of Christ. In my opinion, this principle is but the logical consequence of the other principle: God is infinite love. Christ has been willed by God the Father because, as infinite love, he wants to be loved infinitely. The reason is obvious. The whole of creation is permeated by love. The creation of intelligent beings is not only an act of love; but, in the words of St. Bonaventure, it is a desire to be loved. Now this love could be rendered to God only by the Incarnate Word, since he alone is able to love and glorify God to the supreme degree, that is, in an adequate and infinite measure worthy of the Father of all goodness (*"totius bonitatis"*). It follows, then, by necessity that Christ is the first-willed among all creatures (*"primum volitum inter omnia creatura volita"*).[75] He is also the foundation and ultimate reason for the eternal decree of God which is manifested and actualized in the universe.

I do not want to go any further, Father, but you can see for yourself that if we make just one more step in the application of this principle, we are at the threshold of the doctrine of the Immaculate Conception of the Mother of the Incarnate Word: *"Tu sola a Lui festi ritorno, / ornata del primo suo dono. / Te sola più sù del perdono / l'Amor che può tutto locò."* (You alone have returned to him, / adorned with the first gift. / You alone the all-powerful Love / has placed above all need of forgiveness. — Alessandro Manzoni)[76]

L'Amor che può tutto, l'Amor che il ciel governa (The Love that is all-powerful, the Love that rules the heavens): it is because they refused to listen to this truth that the Jews and the Mohammedans do not accept the mystery of the Incarnation, just as the lack of faith in the infinite Love is, in my opinion, the principal cause of Arianism, Calvinism, Jansenism, and Modernism.

Teilhard. I agree with you, Father, that that is the principal cause. However, you will admit that there are other, perhaps more immediate causes of those erroneous systems. [After a diversion on Jansenism, Père Teilhard said: I see now in a new light the cult of the Sacred Heart of Jesus and of Christ the King: *"Cor Jesu, in quo Pater sibi bene complacuit!"* — (Heart of Jesus, in whom the Father was well pleased!)] But continue, I beg you.

Allegra. Scotus' third theme is: "All the texts of Sacred Scripture and of the Fathers that seem to assert the contrary view — namely, that Christ would not have become man if Adam had not sinned — can be explained in the sense that, if man had not fallen, Christ would not have come as a Redeemer. Perhaps, too, he would not have come in passible or suffering flesh, since there would have been no need for the soul of Christ, predestined by God to such a great glory, to be united with a passible body." In this statement we have something like Scotus' synthesis of the two data of revelation: the absolute primacy of Christ as the primary purpose of the Incarnation, and the Redemption of mankind as its secondary purpose. However, this synthesis had already been made in his prophetic-oracular style by St. Paul, who at one and the same time preached that Christ is King of the whole universe (*Rex totius universitatis*) and that Jesus has been crucified for us.

If there is something for which Scotus ought to be blamed — this blame, as Grabmann has pointed out, involves the entire Scholastic method — it is the attempt to prove his thesis through theological reasoning rather than from Scripture and Tradition. However, one must not forget that the *ratio theologica* represents for Scotus, as for all other great medieval masters, the conclusion of his daily and lofty meditations on Scripture and the Fathers. It was not until the sixteenth century that his disciples began to use the method of biblico-patristic research. This new approach to the problem at issue has already given wonderful results, although much remains to be done in this respect. Two works that come to my mind at this moment as representative of the new approach are those of Ugo Lattanzi, *Il primato universale di Cristo secondo le S. Scritture*,[77] and of Irenée Hausherr, "Un précurseur de la théorie scotiste sur la fin de l'Incarnation: Isaac de Ninive."[78]

I am convinced that within the Scotistic synthesis both Christian anthropology and the mystery of the Cross are preserved in their entirety, and that nothing of the revealed truth is lost or weakened. I might even say that the mystery of the Cross receives a new emphasis by being immersed, as it were, in the purest and most ardent flames of divine love. For, as Scotus argues — like a new John of Patmos — since on the one hand a finite creature cannot by sinning commit an offense of infinite malice, and since on the other hand it would have been enough for our reconciliation with God that the Word should assume through the Incarnation a passible flesh, or, if God had so disposed, that an angel or even a man sustained by divine grace should have satisfied for us, it follows that the sufferings of the crucified Son of God were willed by God to impel us to love him and to realize how greatly we are bound to him (*"ad alliciendum nos ad amorem suum ... et quia voluit hominem amplius teneri Deo"*). In other words, the sufferings of Christ have been willed by his heavenly Father to draw man closer to himself so that he may love him more intensively. That is why, Scotus continues, no salvific grace is ever granted by the Most Holy Trinity to man in his present state except by the merits of Christ's oblation on the Cross, the sacrifice of the Father's most beloved Son out of supreme and infinite love.

In such a synthesis Christ is always and everywhere the First and holds the primacy in everything—*proteuon en pasin*. His sacred humanity, which manifests itself in the sweet and loving mysteries of Bethlehem, Nazareth, Calvary, and the Eucharist, and which shines particularly in the glorious mysteries of the Resurrection, Ascension, and Pentecost, as well as in the glory of his Immaculate Mother and his Church, draws with an irresistible attraction the hearts of men to the love of his Father and of himself, his Mother, and his Church. For, to quote once more Scotus' text, *"Ad alliciendum nos ad amorem suum sic fecit . . . ; et quia voluit nos amplius teneri Deo . . . , ideo multum tenemur ei"* (He so acted in order to impel us to love him . . . ; and since he willed that we be more and more bound to God . . . , we are thus greatly indebted to him).

Teilhard. These words have all the flavor of a liturgical hymn.

Allegra. Father, you are neither the first nor the only one to feel the poetic harmony hidden under the austere rhythm of this passage written in a vigorous but unadorned Latin. If I well recall, Henri Bremond, Levasti, and Portaluppi often point out the poetic rhythm that is contained even in the prose of the mystical writers. As far as Scotus is concerned, such a poetic and spiritual rhythm is more evident in the prayers of his *De primo principio*,[79] but it is no doubt also present in this page of profound theological speculation. This has been noticed by others, too. Thus Signora Varaschini has compared this passage of Scotus to one of those hymns which, according to Pliny, the Christians of Bithynia used to sing to Christ: *"dicere carmen Christo quasi Deo."* My dear friend Bertrand de Margerie, after having asked me for an explanation of the Christological hymns of the New Testament and having read the passage in question, came out with this spontaneous remark: "If we leave aside its external rhythm, this passage of Scotus on Christ, King and Redeemer, seems to me very similar to those hymns of the New Testament. I will speak of this to my mother, who is very much interested in religious poetry." I do not know as yet the reaction of Madame de Margerie, a deeply religious and devout Russian convert, but it is worth noting that a young man like Bertrand, who is a fervent Christian and intends to enter the Society of Jesus,[80] had the same sentiments as Signora Varaschini and many others.

Teilhard. I see, Father Allegra, that you know how to obey your Minister General who, according to what you have told me, a few years ago called upon all the Franciscans to propagate, spread, and defend the doctrine of the primacy of Christ. I congratulate you on this and I beg you to continue to propagate this doctrine with the same passion and the same deep conviction that you have shown to me today.

Allegra. As far as passion and conviction are concerned, I am sure, my dear Père Teilhard, that you can beat me, and by far!

Teilhard. Well, Father, in a sense I think that is true; I must say, however, that this is a defect that is common to both of us. Although traveling different paths, we tend toward the same goal, that is, the source of light and fire which is *le Grand Christ*. But I realize that I always interrupt you. Please continue.

Allegra. Père Teilhard, your expression "the source of light and fire" reminds me of another expression of St. Francis of Assisi: *"ignita et melliflua vis amoris Dei"* (the fiery and sweet force of the love of God).[81] Don't you think that this expression is very appropriate to the Heart of Jesus and the Holy Spirit? But this time it is I who wander; I must conclude now and come to the end of my notes.

In the light of the doctrine we have just been discussing and which has as its background the Christocentric thesis, you can see, Father, that the drama of Redemption is changed from a drama of justice into a drama of the purest and most ardent love. It seems to me — and I wish I had the time and the ability to write on this subject — that the plan of justice is thus superseded by a plan of salvation that in itself is perfect and exempt from any external influence. This plan is rooted solely in the love that God the Father has for his Son and in the love that the Incarnate Son, Jesus Christ, has for his Father and for man. I find support for this view in St. Paul, who affirms that "Jesus endured the cross, disregarding the shamefulness of it" (Heb. 12:2), for the love of his Father and of his brethren. I am also of the opinion that in the light of these doctrines, i. e., the Christocentric doctrine and the doctrine of Redemption out of pure love, it becomes easier to explain the Immaculate Conception of Mary and the value of her sufferings as Co-redemptrix of mankind. Finally, the practical conclusion to be drawn for us is that we should strive to carry into action that simple but forceful corollary: *"Ideo multum tenemur ei"* (We are therefore greatly indebted to him). To quote once more from Scaramuzzi's translation of Scotus' text: "For this reason we are greatly indebted to Christ. We could have been redeemed otherwise, but he has freely chosen to redeem us in this manner. We are therefore indebted to him to a greater degree than if it had been necessary to redeem us in this way without any other alternative. I believe he willed to redeem us in this way chiefly because he wanted to bind us to his love and make man better realize how greatly he is indebted to God."[82]

Père Teilhard, I have explained in Scholastic terms what Scotus says of Christ the Alpha and Omega and of Christ the crucified Redeemer. It seems to me that he holds tightly the two rings of the chain and makes a powerful synthesis of the two doctrines, which in the last analysis constitute the one transcendent mystery of Christ.

Teilhard. Tout s'enchaîne et tout se tient! (It is all well-knit and firm!) I want to thank you and ask you to give serious thought to writing on the subject. I am well aware of the tremendous task you have taken upon yourself of translating the Bible into Chinese, but I am confident you will find time to carry out this other work, too, for the glory of Christ. And be sure to spur on other confreres, as well as other people, to meditate on this doctrine and spread it. If I ever return to France, I will speak of this to my friend Père Auguste Valensin. His heart and his mind are made to climb such heights: his heart beats with the love of our Savior. Is there anything else you want to tell me?

Allegra. Just one more thing, Father, and that is to confirm what you wrote for me in the dedication of *The Divine Milieu:* We are both united in Christ Omega.

Teilhard. A la plus grande gloire du Grand Christ! (To the greatest glory of the Great Christ!)

CONCLUSION

In May, 1945, after the surrender of Germany, I saw Père Teilhard for the last time; it was our farewell meeting.

Teilhard. Father Allegra, I think that we shall soon have to part company. I hope you will pray for me; won't you? I want to thank you once more for your warm friendship and for those intimate hours we have passed together.

Allegra. Père Teilhard, do you remember the young poet Wang-Po, of whom I spoke to you so many times during our digressions on Chinese lyric poetry? Well, I would like to bid you farewell with one of his couplets, which I translate freely:

> Even if you go to the bottom of the sea.
> or to the ends of heaven,
> I will always be near you.

Teilhard. Thank you, Father; thank you again for everything, *mais surtout priez pour moi* (but above all pray for me).

This, I think, is all that need be said here.

Père Teilhard left Peking. I followed his activity from afar, as I was kept informed of it by my Jesuit friends, until the day of his death, which occurred on Easter evening, 1955, in New

York. I received the news at Jerusalem, almost two weeks after the tragic event. It is a well-known fact that within a short time after his death the renowned Jesuit scientist had literally conquered the world. His old Peking friend has silently followed the continuous growth of his fame, but with no excessive enthusiasm for all that has been, and is still being, published about him.

To me his vivid and indelible memory is sufficient. However, I cannot fail to notice that, just as during his lifetime, Teilhard de Chardin continues even after his death to be a sign of contradiction. While his admirers praise his thought to the skies, others look at it with mixed feelings, if not with disdain. It must be admitted that in the somber atmosphere created by existentialist philosophy after the second World War Teilhard's overoptimistic message was likely to fascinate, as it still fascinates today, millions of people. Yet it is my conviction — I say this with the same frankness that was so pleasing to Père Teilhard — that he never thought for a moment of presenting his message as a "creed" to be accepted almost blindly, as seems to be the case with many of his followers today. He rather conceived of his message as an "essay," or better, a milieu or setting that would serve as a starting point for the study of the phenomenon of man in an ascent to the Omega point, *le Grand Christ*. Père Teilhard was and wanted to be considered a pioneer rather than a teacher. It is therefore an offense against his lofty and noble character both to extol him like a mythical figure and to defame him.

To confine myself to my field of competence, I would invite both philosophers and theologians, but especially the latter, to investigate the extent to which the thought of Père Teilhard on the "Great Christ" or Christ as Alpha and Omega can, or perhaps ought to, be integrated into a cosmic vision of the theology of the Incarnation and Redemption out of pure love. If through such research and theological investigation the doctrine of Christ's absolute primacy will be more widely asserted in the Church, I am sure that one of the most earnest desires of the unforgettable Père Teilhard, poet, thinker, and mystic, would have been fulfilled.

Hong Kong, June 24—
Macao, July 10, 1966

TRANSLATOR'S NOTES

[1] In Teilhard de Chardin the study of the phenomenon has a much wider meaning than it has for a natural scientist, who confines himself to the investigation of a particular aspect of reality through empirical observation and the experimental method. Teilhard's phenomenology is an attempt to study the world in its totality in order to discover its structure and its inner dynamics and orientation. It goes further and deeper than the natural sciences and comes closer to philosophy and theology, although, strictly speaking, it is neither of these two latter sciences. For an understanding of Teilhard's phenomenology and its relationship to the natural sciences, philosophy, and theology see N. M. Wildiers, *An Introduction to Teilhard de Chardin*, trans. by Hubert Hoskins (New York: Harper and Row, 1968). This small and unpretentious book is also a most suitable introduction to the thought of Teilhard de Chardin as a whole.

[2] In a letter to the translator, Father Allegra has confirmed that he was the first to use the expression "cosmic theology," which was later popularized by Teilhard and his commentators but with a somewhat different meaning.

[3] Commenting on this point, Father Allegra told me that it seemed inconceivable to Père Teilhard that the universe, that is, the whole of creation, would not be centered on one idea or unifying principle. This principle, in Teilhard's view, could be none other than Christ, the Alpha and Omega.

[4] Jean Guitton, philosopher and writer, is a member of the French Academy. He was the first Catholic layman to be invited to attend the Second Vatican Council.

[5] Père Guillaume Pouget (1847-1933), a learned priest of the Congregation of the Mission founded by St. Vincent

de Paul, has been called a "modern Socrates" by Paul Claudel. His life has been described by Dorothy Poulain in the *Catholic World*, CLXXXI (Aug., 1955), 326-331. The work of Jean Guitton to which Father Allegra refers is *Dialogues avec monsieur Pouget sur la pluralité des mondes, le Christ des évangiles et l'avenir de notre espèce* (Paris: Grasset, 1954). The work has been translated into English by Fergus Murphy and published under the title *Abbé Pouget Discourses* (Baltimore, Md.: Helicon Press, 1959).

[6] Père Auguste Valensin, S. J. (1879-1953), a schoolmate of Teilhard, is the author of *Le christianisme de Dante* (Paris: Aubier, 1954). He studied philosophy under Maurice Blondel and contributed to the exchange of ideas between him and Teilhard. Cf. Henri de Lubac, *Blondel et Teilhard de Chardin* (Paris: Beauchesne, 1965). This work has been translated into English by William Whitman and published under the title *Pierre Teilhard de Chardin and Maurice Blondel: Correspondence* (New York: Herder and Herder, 1967).

[7] Cf. Diomede Scaramuzzi, O. F. M., *Duns Scoto: Summula. Scelta di scritti coordinati in dottrina*, Edizioni "Testi Cristiani" (Florence: Libreria Editrice Fiorentina, 1932). This is a collection of texts from Scotus' works with an Italian translation.

[8] Cf. Parthenius Minges, O. F. M., *Ioannis Duns Scoti doctrina philosophica et theologica*, 2 vols. (Quaracchi: Typographia Collegii S. Bonaventurae, 1930). In this work the author has not only collected an impressive amount of Scotus' texts on most philosophical and theological subjects, but has also organized them systematically and commented upon them.

[9] Cf. John Duns Scotus, *A Treatise on God as First Principle*, trans. and ed. by Allan B. Wolter, O. F. M. (Chicago: Franciscan Herald Press, 1966), p. 145: "Tu bonus sine termino, bonitatis tuae radios liberalissime com-

TRANSLATOR'S NOTES

municans, ad quem amabilissimum singula suo modo recurrunt ut ad ultimum suum finem."

[10] As previously stated (cf. p. 24, above), *Le milieu divin* was later published both in French and in English. Teilhard's note *Sur la notion de la perfection chrétienne*, which contains several interesting marginal schematic drawings by Teilhard himself, is still unpublished, while his message *La parole attendue* has been published in French but not in English. Cf. *Cahiers Pierre Teilhard de Chardin*, No. 4: *La parole attendue* (Paris: Editions du Seuil, 1963), pp. 22-29.

For a popular presentation in English of the doctrine of the absolute primacy of Christ, see Michael D. Meilach, O. F. M., *The Primacy of Christ in Doctrine and Life* (Chicago: Franciscan Herald Press, 1964). This work has appeared in a new revised edition under the title *From Order to Omega* (Chicago: Franciscan Herald Press, 1966).

A scholarly and comprehensive study of the absolute primacy of Christ from the viewpoint of Scripture and Tradition is found in Jean-François Bonnefoy, O. F. M., *Christ and the Cosmos*, trans. and ed. by Michael D. Meilach, O. F. M. (Paterson, N. J.: St. Anthony Guild Press, 1965).

[11] Adhémar d'Alès, S. J. (1861-1938), was a French theologian and patrologist who inaugurated with Père Bainvel the periodical *Bibliothèque de théologie historique* and served as principal director of the *Dictionnaire apologétique de la foi catholique*, 4 vols. (Paris: Beauchesne, 1911-1922).

[12] Léonce de Grandmaison, S. J. (1868-1927), was the principal founder of the periodical *Recherches de science religieuse* and the author, among other works, of *Jesus Christ: His Person, His Message, His Credentials*, trans. by Dom Basil Whelan, Ada Lane, and Douglas Carter, 3 vols. (New York: Sheed and Ward, 1930-1934). He was one of the few professors of theology admired by Teilhard, who

used to call him "the divine Léonce." See Claude Cuénot, *Teilhard de Chardin: A Biographical Study* (Baltimore, Md.: Helicon, 1965), p. 13.

[13] Jules Lebreton, S. J. (1873-1956), was a French theologian and church historian who founded with Léonce de Grandmaison the periodical *Recherches de science religieuse*.

[14] Francisco Suárez (1548-1617), a leading Jesuit philosopher and theologian, proposed the theory of a twofold reason for the Incarnation: one absolute, which is the excellence of the Incarnation itself; and one relative, which is the Redemption of mankind conditioned by Adam's sin.

[15] Cf. A. Michel, "Incarnation," *Dictionnaire de théologie catholique*, Vol. VII (2), cols. 1445-1539.

[16] Cf. Leonardo M. Bello, O. F. M., "Litterae encyclicae de universali Christi primatu atque regalitate," *Acta Ordinis Fratrum Minorum*, LII (1933), 293-311.

[17] Brooke Foss Westcott (1825-1901), an Anglican Scripture scholar and bishop, is the author of numerous books and articles. Among his best-known works are: *A General Survey of the History of the Canon of the New Testament* (7th ed.; London: Macmillan, 1896); *An Introduction to the Study of the Gospels* (7th ed.; London: Macmillan, 1888).

[18] Bishop Michel d'Herbigny, S. J., was named by Pope Pius XI first President of the Pontifical Commission for Russia after the Commission was separated from the Sacred Congregation for the Oriental Church on April 6, 1930. He was also named Honorary President of the Pontifical Institute of Oriental Studies.

[19] Père Chrysostome Urrutibéhéty, O. F. M., devoted almost his entire life to the popularization of the doctrine of the absolute primacy of Christ and the devotion to Christ

the King. His principal work is *Christus, Alpha et Omega, seu de Christi universali regno* (2nd ed.; Lille: Girard, 1910).

[20] The teaching of these Fathers of the Church on the primacy of Christ has been discussed by Dominic J. Unger, O. F. M. Cap., in several articles that appeared in *Franciscan Studies* between 1945 and 1949, each dealing with an individual Father.

[21] Rupert (d. 1135), abbot of Deutz, near Cologne, Germany, expounds his thought on the motive of Christ's Incarnation in his treatise *De gloria et honore Filii Hominis, lib. 13* (Migne, *Patrologia Latina*, Vol. CLXVIII, cols. 1624-1629).

[22] Cf. St. Bernardine of Siena, "De universali regno et dominio Jesu Christi," *Opera omnia* (Quaracchi: Typographia Collegii S. Bonaventurae, 1950-1965), II, 340-352.

[23] Cf. St. Lawrence of Brindisi, "Sermo I super: Missus est, n. 4, *Opera omnia* (Padua: Ex Officina Typographica Seminarii, 1928), I, 80. See also Dominic J. Unger, O. F. M. Cap., "The Absolute Primacy of Christ and His Virgin Mother according to St. Lawrence of Brindisi," *Collectanea franciscana*, XXII (1952), 113-119.

[24] A strong defender of Scotus' Christocentric doctrine, Père Déodat Marie de Basly, O. F. M., is best known for his work *Pourquoi Jésus-Christ?* (Paris: Desclée de Brouwer, 1903), which has had several editions.

[25] Père Valentin Marie Breton, O. F. M. (1877-1957), is the author of several studies on Franciscan spirituality. The following are available in English: *Franciscan Spirituality*, trans. by F. Frey, O. F. M. (Chicago: Franciscan Herald Press, 1957); *In Christ's Company*, trans. by Michael D. Meilach, O. F. M. (Chicago: Franciscan Herald Press, 1961).

TRANSLATOR'S NOTES

²⁶ Père Marie Bonaventure (Pasquier), O. F. M., published *L'eucharistie et le mystère du Christ d'après l'Ecriture et la Tradition* (Paris: Poussielgue, 1897), an extensive study in which Christ is discussed in relation to the Eucharist.

²⁷ Père Jean François Bonnefoy, O. F. M. (1897-1958), is the author of many scholarly studies, including *Christ and the Cosmos* (see note 10, paragraph 3) and *The Immaculate Conception in the Divine Plan*, trans. by Michael D. Meilach, O. F. M. (Paterson, N. J.: St. Anthony Guild Press, 1967).

²⁸ Père Jean-Marie Bissen, O. F. M. (1890-1939), published several articles on the doctrine of Christ's primacy, among which it is worth mentioning "De praedestinatione absoluta Christi secundum Duns Scotum expositio doctrinalis," *Antonianum*, XII (1947), 3-36.

²⁹ Père Ephrem Longpré, O. F. M. (1890-1965), wrote extensively in the field of Franciscan theology and was a strong promoter of the doctrine of the absolute primacy of Christ. Chief among his studies are: "Le Bx. Duns Scot, Docteur du Verbe Incarné," *France Franciscaine*, XVII (1934), 1-36; *The Kingship of Jesus Christ according to Saint Bonaventure and Blessed John Duns Scotus*, trans. by D. J. Barry, O. F. M. (Paterson, N. J.: St. Anthony Guild Press, 1944); "La primauté du Christ," *Lumières d'Assise*, I (1947), 27-38.

³⁰ Father Charles Balić, O. F. M., a world-renowned Scotist and Mariologist, has contributed more than anyone else to the development of Scotistic studies in the last thirty years. He was the chief organizer of the International Scotistic Congress held at Oxford and Edinburgh in September, 1966, whose proceedings have been published in four large volumes under the title *De doctrina Ioannis Duns Scoti* (Rome: Commissio Scotistica, 1968).

[31] Father Agostino Gemelli, O. F. M. (1878-1959), was the founder of Sacred Heart University in Milan, Italy, and was appointed rector for his lifetime. A recognized authority in psychology, he devoted a considerable part of his activity to Franciscan studies and became the chief promoter of the doctrine of the Kingship of Christ, which won the official recognition of the Catholic Church. One of Gemelli's outstanding works is *The Franciscan Message to the World*, trans. and adapted by Henry Louis Hughes (London: Burns Oates and Washbourne, 1934).

[32] Pierre Cardinal de Bérulle (1575-1629) was the founder of the French Oratory and a leading figure in the French school of spirituality. Pope Urban VIII called him "the apostle of the Incarnate Word."

[33] Jean Jacques Olier (1608-1657) was the founder of the Society of St. Sulpice (the Sulpicians), whose main purpose is to prepare young men for the priesthood. He was also a leader in the French school of spirituality.

[34] Louis-Victor-Emile Bougaud (1823-1888), French bishop, orator, and writer, is the author of *Le christianisme et les temps présents*, 5 vols. (8th ed.; Paris: Poussielgue, 1901).

[35] Geremia Bonomelli (1831-1914), bishop of Cremona from 1871 to his death and author of numerous articles and books on a variety of topics, defended the Scotistic doctrine that the Incarnation of the Word is the central event in the present divine economy.

[36] Frederick William Faber (1814-1863) was an English Oratorian and a popular spiritual writer. One of his latest works, *Bethlehem* (New ed.; Philadelphia: Reilly, 1955), is a study of the Incarnation along the lines of Cardinal de Bérulle's thought.

[37] See note 17 above.

[38] Matthias Joseph Scheeben (1835-1888) shows his adherence to the Scotistic doctrine of Christ's absolute primacy in *The Mysteries of Christianity*, trans. by Cyril Vollert, S. J. (St. Louis: Herder, 1946). See the section on "The Mystery of the God-Man and His Economy," pp. 311-465.

[39] Professor Carmelo Ottaviano, a graduate of Sacred Heart University, Milan, is the founder of *Sophia*, a philosophical review, and the author of a considerable number of studies in philosophy and the history of philosophy.

[40] St. Francis de Sales (1567-1622) emphasizes the absolute primacy of Christ in his treatise *On the Love of God*, trans. by John K. Ryan (Garden City, N. Y.: Doubleday, 1963), Vol. I, Book 2, Chaps. IV and V, pp. 111-116.

[41] Gerard Manley Hopkins (1844-1889), a convert to Catholicism and a member of the Society of Jesus, is a well-known English poet who became greatly interested in the thought of Duns Scotus, and especially in his theology of the Incarnation. "Duns Scotus' Oxford" is no. 44 in *The Poems of Gerard Manley Hopkins*, edited by W. H. Gardner and N. H. MacKenzie (4th ed.; London: Oxford University Press, 1967). For a study of Scotus' influence on Hopkins, see Robert R. Boyle, S. J., "Duns Scotus in the Poetry of Hopkins," in *Scotus Speaks Today: 1266-1966. Seventh Centenary Symposium* (Southfield, Mich.: Duns Scotus College, 1968), pp. 297-319.

[42] See note 40 above.

[43] Father Allegra refers to Gemelli's work *The Franciscan Message to the World*, mentioned in note 31 above.

[44] In his work *The True Life: Sociology of the Supernatural*, trans. by Barbara B. Carter (Paterson, N. J.: St. Anthony Guild Press, 1943), Don Luigi Sturzo (1871-1959) portrays a world order in which the Incarnation takes on its full historical meaning.

[45] A prominent contemporary theologian favoring the Scotistic doctrine on the primary end of the Incarnation is Karl Rahner, S. J. See his *Theological Investigations*, trans. by E. Ernst, O. P. (Baltimore, Md.: Helicon, 1961), I, 164-166. The issue is considered of paramount importance by Hans Urs von Balthasar, *A Theology of History* (New York: Sheed and Ward, 1963), pp. 61-63, and by Charles Davis, *Theology for Today* (New York: Sheed and Ward, 1962), pp. 159-170.

[46] This is a free quotation from John Duns Scotus, *Reportata Parisiensia* III, dist. 7, quaest. 4, n. 5 (Vivès edition, XXIII, 303b).

[47] Cf. John Duns Scotus, *Opus Oxoniense*, I, dist. 17, quaest. 3, n. 31 (Vivès edition, X, 93a). See also note 65 below for information on the *Opus Oxoniense*.

[48] For information on Père Marie Bonaventure, Olier, and Faber, see notes 26, 33, and 36, respectively. Charles Louis Gay (1815-1892) was a French theologian and writer who belonged to the Oratorian school of spirituality and who, like Faber, followed the general lines of Pierre de Bérulle's thought.

[49] See note 6 above.

[50] This and the following translations of Dante's *Paradiso* are taken from Dante Alighieri, *The Divine Comedy: A New Prose Translation*, with an introduction and notes by H. R. Huse (New York-Toronto: Rinehart, 1954).

[51] This statement is taken from the *Legenda antiqua S. Francisci*. See *The Words of St. Francis*, ed. by James Meyer, O. F. M. (Chicago: Franciscan Herald Press, 1966), p. 93, where the full text with a slightly different translation is reproduced: "Courtesy is one of the properties of the Lord, who serves out sun and rain and all the things which we need for our life, to the just and the unjust alike.

121

TRANSLATOR'S NOTES

For Courtesy is a sister of Charity, and she extinguishes hatred and keeps Charity alive."

⁵² Gulielmus Estius (1542-1613), a Dutch exegete and theologian whom Pope Benedict XIV called *Doctor fundatissimus*, is the author of a commentary on the New Testament epistles entitled *In omnes beati Pauli et septem catholicas apostolorum epistolas commentarii* (Douai, 1614-1616).

⁵³ For a discussion of the scriptural and theological issues raised by Father Allegra, see Bonnefoy, *Christ and the Cosmas*, Part II, Chap. I, art. 3: "Christ the Firstborn of All Creation," pp. 146-172; *ibid.*, art. 4: "Christ the Model, Principle, and End of All Things," pp. 172-181; *ibid.*, Chap. II, art. 3: "Christ the Redeemer," pp. 228-246.

⁵⁴ The Iranists are those scholars in the early part of this century who stressed the influence of Persian doctrine on Judaism and Christianity, apparently without sufficient justification.

⁵⁵ *The Divine Comedy: Paradiso*, XXII, 42.

⁵⁶ Père Pierre Charles, S. J. (1883-1954), whom Teilhard used to call "the great Pierre Charles," was professor of missiology both at Louvain University, Belgium, and the Gregorian University in Rome. He is the author of various works on missiology and ascetical theology, among which is *La prière de toutes les heures* mentioned by Father Allegra. This work has been translated into English by Maud Monahan and published under the title *Prayer for All Times* (Westminster, Md.: Newman Press, 1949). Père Charles constantly tried, but without success, to have Teilhard's works published, especially *Le milieu divin*. Reportedly he inspired the discussion "On the Place and Part of Evil in a World in Evolution" which was added as an appendix to Teilhard's *The Phenomenon of Man*. Cf. Cuénot, *Teilhard de Chardin*, p. 6, n. 8, and p. 13.

57 Joseph Huby, S. J. (1878-1948), a French apologist and spiritual writer who was a colleague and then an heir of Léonce de Grandmaison (cf. note 12), seems to favor the Scotistic interpretation of St. Paul in his work *Saint Paul: Les Epîtres de la captivité* (14th ed.; Paris: Beauchesne, 1947). One of Huby's best-known works is *Christus: Manuel d'histoire des religions* (Paris: Beauchesne, 1912), which is mentioned by Father Allegra.

58 *Quodlibet* or *Quaestiones quodlibetales* was the name given to the disputations held twice a year, i. e., at the Easter and Christmas seasons, in the medieval universities, and especially at the University of Paris. The disputations were open to the public, and since no particular topic was assigned, the participants could question the Master on any subject: hence the term *disputationes de quolibet*. By contrast, the *Quaestiones disputatae* were the regular disputations held during the year in which the Master proposed and developed a particular topic and answered the objections raised by the students.

59 Cf. Vol. XII (2), cols. 2520-2536. The article "Polygénisme" was written by A. and J. Bouyssonie.

60 Since the time of Father Allegra's conversations with Père Teilhard, much has been written on original sin, and attempts have been made, even by Catholic theologians and exegetes, to interpret the Bible teaching in accord with the theory of evolution and polygenism. For an assessment of these views, see the *New Catholic Encyclopedia* (1967), under "Original Sin," X, 776-781; "Evolution, Human," V, 676-685; "Polygenism," XI, 539-540.

61 Teilhard's special interest in Voltaire may be due, among other things, to the fact that he was remotely related to him through his mother. Cf. Cuénot, *Teilhard de Chardin*, p. 1.

⁶² Cf. St. Bonaventure, *Opera omnia* (Quaracchi: Typographia Collegii S. Bonaventurae, 1882-1902), VI, 16: "Verbum divinum est omnis creatura, quia Deum loquitur."

⁶³ Cf. *Encyclopaedia of Religion and Ethics*, IV (1920), 398, wherein Edmund G. Gardner quotes Manning's statement. Henry Edward Cardinal Manning (1808-1892), a convert from the Anglican ministry, became a Catholic priest in 1851 and was named archbishop of Westminster in 1865. His works include *The Eternal Priesthood* (Baltimore, Md.: Murphy, 1883) and *Religio viatoris* (3rd ed.; London: Burns and Oates, 1888).

⁶⁴ For the English translation of Scotus' *De primo principio*, see note 9 above.

⁶⁵ "Deus est formaliter dilectio et formaliter charitas, et non tantum effective." This text is taken from Duns Scotus' *Opus Oxoniense*, I, dist. 17, quaest. 3, n. 31 (Vivès edition, X, 93a). The *Opus Oxoniense* contains Scotus' commentary on the *Book of Sentences* of Peter Lombard at the University of Oxford. It is Scotus' most important and reliable work. In the critical edition of the *Opus Oxoniense*, which goes under the name of *Ordinatio* — the title given to it by Scotus himself after he revised and "ordered" (i. e., reorganized) the material of his lectures — the above text reads: "Deus est formaliter caritas et dilectio, non tantum effective." *Ord.* I, dist. 17, pars 1, quaest. 1-2, n. 173 (Vatican edition, V, 222).

⁶⁶ "Conceptus entis infiniti virtualiter plura includit; sicut enim ens includit virtualiter bonum et verum in se, ita ens infinitum includit verum infinitum et bonum infinitum et omnem perfectionem simpliciter sub ratione infiniti." *Opus Oxon.*, I, dist. 3, quaest. 2, n. 17 (Vivès edition, IX, 33b); *Ord.* I, dist. 3, pars 1, quaest. 1-2 (Vatican edition, III, 40-41).

[67] "Summum Dei opus non potest esse occasionatum." *Opus Oxon.*, III, dist. 7, quaest. 3, n. 3 (Vivès edition, XIV, 355a).

[68] "Deus voluit se diligi ab alio, qui potest eum summe diligere." *Reportata Parisiensia* III, dist. 7, quaest. 4, n. 5 (Vivès edition, XXIII, 303b).

[69] "Omnes auctoritates possunt exponi sic, scilicet quod Christus non venisset ut Redemptor, nisi homo cecidisset." *Opus Oxon.*, III, dist. 7, quaest. 3, n. 3 (Vivès edition, XIV, 355a).

[70] "Tunc dico quod omnia huiusmodi quae facta sunt a Christo circa redemptionem nostram, non fuerunt necessaria, nisi praesupposita ordinatione divina, quae sic ordinavit fieri, et tunc tantum necessitate consequentiae necessarium fuit Christum pati. . . . Et ideo multum tenemur ei. Ex quo enim aliter potuisset homo redimi et tamen ex sua libera voluntate sic redemit, multum ei tenemur, et amplius quam si sic necessario et non aliter potuissemus fuisse redempti; ideo ad alliciendum nos ad amorem suum, ut credo, hoc praecipue fecit, et quia voluit hominem amplius teneri Deo." *Opus Oxon.*, III, dist. 20, quaest. unica, n. 10 (Vivès edition, XIV, 737b-738a).

[71] "Ergo Trinitas nullum adiutorium pertinens ad salutem contulit homini viatori, nisi in virtute huius oblationis Christi in cruce factae et a persona dilectissima et ex maxima charitate." *Opus Oxon.*, IV, dist. 2, quaest. 1, n. 7 (Vivès edition, XVI, 246b).

[72] Cf. Frederick W. Faber, *The Blessed Sacrament* (New ed.; Philadelphia: Reilly, 1958), p. 338.

[73] Cf. Scaramuzzi, *Duns Scoto: Summula*, p. 185, n. 2.

[74] St. Augustine, *Tractatus in Ioannis Evangelium*, XXVI, n. 4 (Migne, *Patrologia Latina*, Vol. XXXV, col. 1608).

TRANSLATOR'S NOTES

[75] Cf. John Duns Scotus, *Reportata Barcinonensia* III, dist. 7, quaest. 3, in Carolus Balić, O. F. M., *Theologiae Marianae elementa* (Sibenik: Typographia Kačic, 1933), p. 184.

[76] This stanza is taken from Manzoni's poem "Ognissanti." See *Tutte le poesie di Alessandro Manzoni*, ed. by Giovanni Titta Rosa (Milan: Casa Editrice Ceschina, 1966), p. 219.

[77] (Rome: Lateranum, 1937.) Lattanzi's work is an exegetical study of the universal primacy of Christ according to Scotus' doctrine.

[78] Cf. *Recherches de science religieuse*, XXII (1932), 316-320. In his study Irenée Hausherr, S. J., shows that Isaac the Ninevite, a seventh-century Nestorian, has anticipated the Scotistic doctrine on the primary motive of the Incarnation in his work *De perfectione religiosa*, ed. by P. Bedjan, C. M. (Paris, 1909), pp. 583-586.

[79] Cf. *A Treatise on God as First Principle*, pp. 2, 43, 71, 143-147, 151.

[80] Bertrand de Margerie did actually become a Jesuit priest and went as a missionary to Brazil.

[81] This expression is contained in St. Francis' prayer "Absorbeat," so named from its first word. Cf. *Opuscula Sancti Patris Francisci Assisiensis* (Quaracchi: Typographia Collegii S. Bonaventurae, 1949), p. 125.

[82] Scaramuzzi, *Duns Scoto: Summula*, p. 183.